Constitutional Law: Principles and Practice in Modern Democracies

In the complex tapestry of modern governance, constitutional law stands as the bedrock of democratic societies, shaping the very essence of their existence. At the heart of this legal framework lies the constitution, a living document that embodies the values, aspirations, and fundamental rights of a nation's citizens. "Constitutional Law: Principles and Practice in Modern Democracies" is an exploration of this pivotal branch of law, offering readers a comprehensive and enlightening journey into the foundations, intricacies, and practical applications of constitutional principles in contemporary democracies.

As societies continue to evolve and face new challenges, constitutional law acts as a compass, guiding the way forward and safeguarding the delicate balance between governance and individual freedoms. In this book, we embark on a voyage to understand the essence of constitutionalism, from its historical origins to its relevance in the fast-paced world of the twenty-first century. We delve into the core principles that underpin constitutional law, such as the separation of powers, federalism, judicial review, and the rule of law, examining how they interact to preserve the integrity of democratic institutions.

The journey does not stop at the theoretical realm. Instead, we step into the realm of practice, exploring how constitutional law shapes real-world scenarios. Through insightful case studies and landmark court decisions, we witness constitutional principles in action, shaping pivotal issues such as human rights, equality, free speech, privacy, and social justice. We examine how constitutional courts interpret and apply these principles, striking the delicate balance between protecting individual liberties and promoting the common good.

"Constitutional Law: Principles and Practice in Modern Democracies" is a collaborative effort, woven together by the expertise of legal scholars, practitioners, and policymakers who bring diverse perspectives and experiences to the table. The book embraces the richness and complexities of constitutional law, offering readers a nuanced understanding of the challenges and opportunities faced in its application.

As we embark on this intellectual journey, our goal is not only to illuminate the significance of constitutional law in modern democracies but also to inspire critical thinking and active engagement. We invite readers to explore the dynamic interplay between constitutional principles and the evolving needs of democratic societies. Through this exploration, we hope to foster a deeper appreciation for the profound impact of constitutional law in shaping the course of nations and the lives of their citizens.

In conclusion, "Constitutional Law: Principles and Practice in Modern Democracies" serves as a comprehensive guide, navigating through the profound landscape of constitutional law, and revealing how it continues to uphold the pillars of democracy, empower citizens, and illuminate the path towards a more just and equitable society.

I. Introduction to Constitutional Law

- Definition and Scope of Constitutional Law
- Historical Development of Constitutionalism
- Role of Constitutions in Modern Democracies
- Importance of Constitutional Law in Governance

II. Foundational Principles of Constitutional Law

- The Rule of Law and its Significance
- Separation of Powers: Balancing Government Functions
- Federalism and Distribution of Powers
- Judicial Review: Ensuring Constitutional Supremacy
- Fundamental Rights and Liberties

III. Drafting and Amending Constitutions

- Constituent Assembly and Constitutional Drafting
- Principles of Constitutional Interpretation
- Constitutional Amendments: Procedures and Limitations

IV. Constitutional Institutions and Their Functions

- Executive Branch: Presidential vs. Parliamentary Systems
- Legislative Branch: Bicameralism and Lawmaking
- Judiciary: Structure, Independence, and Judicial Activism
- Role of Constitutional Courts in Protecting Rights

V. Constitutional Principles in Practice: Case Studies

- Freedom of Speech and Expression: Balancing Rights and Responsibilities
- Right to Privacy and Surveillance in the Digital Age
- Equality and Non-Discrimination: Addressing Social Injustices
- Right to Education and Access to Healthcare Services
- Environmental Protection and Sustainable Development
- Electoral Systems and Political Representation

VI. Judicial Review and the Role of the Courts

- Doctrine of Judicial Review and its Limitations
- The Impact of Judicial Decisions on Public Policy
- Court Interpretation of Constitutionally Protected Rights

VII. Protection of Human Rights and Social Justice

- Economic, Social, and Cultural Rights
- Rights of Vulnerable Populations: Women, Children, Minorities, etc.
- Intersectionality of Rights and Multiple Discrimination

VIII. Constitutional Law and Emerging Challenges

- Constitutionalism in the Digital Era
- National Security and Civil Liberties
- Responses to Global Crises: Pandemics, Climate Change, etc.

IX. Comparative Constitutional Law

- Analysis of Different Constitutional Systems
- Lessons from International and Regional Human Rights Courts

X. The Role of Civil Society and Public Engagement

- Importance of Civic Education on Constitutional Rights and Duties
- Citizen Participation in Constitutional Reforms

XI. Future Directions of Constitutional Law

- Adapting Constitutional Law to Technological Advancements
- Ensuring Constitutional Resilience and Flexibility
- Addressing Challenges in a Globalized World

XII. Conclusion:

- Empowering Democratic Societies through Constitutional Law

Definition and Scope of Constitutional Law

Definition: Constitutional law is a branch of public law that deals with the principles, structure, powers, and functions of a country's constitution. It encompasses the legal framework that establishes and governs the fundamental institutions of the state, delineates the distribution of powers among different branches of government, and guarantees the rights and liberties of its citizens. Constitutional law is foundational to a nation's legal system, as it sets the framework for the exercise of governmental authority and ensures the protection of individual rights within a constitutional democracy.

Scope: The scope of constitutional law is extensive, covering a wide range of topics and principles that govern the constitutional order of a nation. Its key elements include:

1. The Constitution: Constitutional law focuses on the study and interpretation of a country's written or unwritten constitution, which serves as the supreme law of the land. The constitution outlines the fundamental principles, values, and structures of the state, including the establishment of government institutions, their functions, and the division of powers.

2. Separation of Powers: Constitutional law addresses the principle of separation of powers, which divides the government into distinct branches – the executive, legislative, and judicial – each with its own functions

and limitations. This division aims to prevent the concentration of power and provide checks and balances to safeguard against abuse of authority.

3. Federalism: In countries with federal systems, constitutional law defines the distribution of powers between the central (national) government and the subnational entities (states, provinces, etc.). It outlines the relationship between these entities and ensures their autonomy within the framework of the national constitution.

4. Judicial Review: One of the essential aspects of constitutional law is the principle of judicial review, which empowers the judiciary to review the constitutionality of laws and government actions. Constitutional courts have the authority to invalidate laws or executive actions that are found to be in violation of the constitution.

5. Fundamental Rights and Liberties: Constitutional law guarantees and protects the fundamental rights and liberties of individuals. It ensures that citizens' rights to freedom of speech, expression, religion, privacy, due process, and equal protection under the law are upheld and not infringed upon by the government.

6. Amendment and Interpretation: The process of amending the constitution and the principles of constitutional interpretation are within the scope of constitutional law. This includes determining how the constitution evolves over time and adapts to changing societal needs and values.

7. Constitutional Governance: Constitutional law addresses the principles and practices of constitutional governance, encompassing issues like presidential and parliamentary systems, electoral systems, and the functioning of government institutions.

8. Constitutional Crisis and Remedies: In the event of

a constitutional crisis or disputes over constitutional interpretation, constitutional law provides mechanisms for resolving these issues, ensuring the stability and continuity of the constitutional order.

Overall, constitutional law is of paramount importance in shaping the nature and functioning of a nation's legal and political systems. It serves as the foundation for democratic governance, ensuring that government actions are constrained by the rule of law and that the rights and freedoms of citizens are protected and respected.

Historical Development of Constitutionalism

The historical development of constitutionalism spans centuries and has evolved in response to various political, social, and philosophical influences. It has been shaped by the need to establish limits on government power, protect individual rights, and create a stable framework for governance. Here is an overview of the key stages in the historical development of constitutionalism:

1. Ancient Roots: The origins of constitutionalism can be traced back to ancient civilizations, such as ancient Greece and Rome. In Athens, for example, the concept of rule of law and the notion of citizen participation in decision-making laid the groundwork for early democratic principles. In Rome, the Twelve Tables (451–450 BCE) established a written code of laws that applied to all citizens, irrespective of their social status.

2. Medieval and Feudal Period: During the medieval period, constitutionalism took a different form in feudal societies. Feudal monarchs, like King John of England, were constrained by agreements such as the Magna Carta (1215), which limited the king's power and established certain rights for the nobility and freemen.

3. Emergence of Parliamentary Sovereignty: In the late medieval and early modern periods, constitutional ideas further developed in Europe. The English

Parliament gained prominence in asserting its authority over the monarchy during the reigns of Henry VIII and Elizabeth I. The English Civil War (1642-1651) and the Glorious Revolution of 1688 led to the establishment of parliamentary supremacy and the supremacy of the law.

4. Enlightenment and Liberal Constitutionalism: The Enlightenment period in the 17th and 18th centuries gave rise to the idea of natural rights and social contract theory. Thinkers like John Locke and Jean-Jacques Rousseau advocated for limited government, popular sovereignty, and the protection of individual liberties. These ideas profoundly influenced the American and French Revolutions, leading to the adoption of foundational documents such as the United States Constitution (1787) and the Declaration of the Rights of Man and of the Citizen (1789).

5. Constitutionalism in the 19th Century: The 19th century witnessed the spread of constitutionalism to various parts of the world. New constitutions were established in many European countries, and constitutional monarchies emerged. The concept of constitutionalism also influenced anti-colonial movements in Latin America and Asia, leading to the creation of constitutional frameworks in independent nations.

6. Twentieth Century and Beyond: The 20th century saw the proliferation of constitutionalism globally, with many countries adopting written constitutions and strengthening the protection of fundamental rights. The Universal Declaration of Human Rights (1948) marked a significant milestone in the international recognition of human rights as essential components of constitutionalism.

7. Supranational and Regional Constitutionalism: In more recent times, the development of supranational

entities, such as the European Union (EU), has given rise to regional constitutionalism. These organizations have their legal frameworks, charters, and treaties, influencing the constitutional landscape at both national and international levels.

Throughout history, constitutionalism has evolved to reflect changing political ideologies and societal values. It has become a central concept in modern democracies, ensuring that governments operate under the rule of law, protect the rights of individuals, and are accountable to the people they govern. As the world continues to change, constitutionalism remains a fundamental pillar of governance, providing stability, predictability, and protection for societies across the globe.

Role of Constitutions in Modern Democracies

The role of constitutions in modern democracies is multifaceted and pivotal. Constitutions serve as the supreme law of the land, providing the framework for the organization and functioning of the state. They play a crucial role in upholding the principles of democratic governance, protecting individual rights and liberties, and ensuring the accountability of government institutions. Here are the key roles of constitutions in modern democracies:

1. Establishing Government Structure: Constitutions outline the structure of the government and its various branches. They delineate the roles and powers of the executive, legislative, and judicial branches, establishing a system of checks and balances to prevent the concentration of power in any one branch.

2. Defining Fundamental Rights and Liberties: Constitutions enshrine fundamental rights and liberties that are inherent to all citizens. These rights include freedom of speech, religion, assembly, and association, as well as due process, equality before the law, and the right to privacy. Constitutions serve as a safeguard against potential abuses of power and protect citizens from arbitrary government actions.

3. Ensuring Rule of Law: Constitutions uphold the principle of the rule of law, which means that all individuals, including government officials, are subject to and bound by the law. This ensures that no

one is above the law and that government actions are based on legal authority.

4. Protecting Minority Rights: Constitutions play a crucial role in protecting the rights of minority groups and individuals. They provide a framework to ensure that the majority cannot unduly oppress or discriminate against minorities.

5. Limiting Government Power: One of the primary functions of constitutions is to establish limits on government power. By defining the scope of governmental authority and providing for the separation of powers, constitutions prevent government overreach and protect against tyranny.

6. Defining Citizenship and National Identity: Constitutions often define who is considered a citizen of the country and outline the rights and responsibilities of citizenship. They also contribute to shaping the national identity and values of a nation.

7. Ensuring Stability and Continuity: Constitutions provide stability and continuity in governance. They set out the basic principles and institutions that endure beyond changes in governments and political leadership.

8. Enabling Constitutional Review: Constitutions establish the framework for constitutional review, allowing courts to assess the constitutionality of laws and government actions. Judicial review ensures that laws and policies are consistent with the constitution and provides a mechanism for challenging actions that violate constitutional rights.

9. Facilitating Constitutional Amendments: Constitutions typically outline procedures for amending the constitution. These processes allow the constitution to adapt to changing societal needs and values without compromising its core principles.

10. Promoting Democratic Governance: Constitutions

reinforce democratic principles by providing mechanisms for free and fair elections, ensuring representation, and fostering public participation in decision-making processes.

In summary, constitutions in modern democracies serve as the cornerstone of governance, shaping the framework within which governments operate and ensuring the protection of individual rights and liberties. They provide the essential rules of the game for democratic societies, promoting stability, justice, and the rule of law while safeguarding against abuses of power. As the embodiment of a nation's values and aspirations, constitutions empower citizens to participate in shaping their collective destiny and hold their governments accountable for upholding the principles of democratic governance.

Importance of Constitutional Law in Governance

Constitutional law holds immense importance in governance, acting as the bedrock of a stable and just society. It plays a central role in shaping the framework of government, guiding the behavior of state institutions, and safeguarding individual rights and liberties. Here are the key reasons why constitutional law is crucial in governance:

1. Establishing Government Structure: Constitutional law defines the structure of government, including the distribution of powers among its branches. This allocation of authority ensures a system of checks and balances, preventing any one branch from becoming too dominant and ensuring accountability in governance.

2. Protecting Individual Rights: Constitutional law enshrines fundamental rights and liberties that are essential for individuals' dignity and well-being. By providing a legal foundation for these rights, it ensures that citizens are protected from government overreach and arbitrary actions.

3. Upholding the Rule of Law: Constitutional law upholds the principle of the rule of law, meaning that all individuals, including government officials, are subject to and bound by the law. It ensures that government actions are consistent with legal norms and that decisions are made impartially and transparently.

4. Promoting Stability and Predictability: Constitutions provide stability and continuity in governance, guiding the functioning of the state regardless of political changes. By establishing fundamental principles and institutions, constitutional law fosters predictability and consistency in the governance process.
5. Facilitating Democratic Governance: Constitutional law lays the foundation for democratic principles, including free and fair elections, representation, and public participation. It ensures that government decisions are made through democratic processes and reflect the will of the people.
6. Limiting Government Power: One of the critical functions of constitutional law is to limit the scope of government power. By establishing the boundaries of governmental authority, constitutions protect against abuses of power and preserve individual liberties.
7. Ensuring Government Accountability: Constitutional law holds government institutions accountable for their actions. The principles of transparency, accountability, and the rule of law allow citizens to scrutinize government decisions and seek redress if their rights are violated.
8. Providing a Legal Framework: Constitutional law provides the legal framework for addressing complex societal issues. It guides the formulation and implementation of policies, regulations, and laws to address public concerns and societal needs.
9. Safeguarding Minority Rights: Constitutional law protects the rights of minority groups and individuals, ensuring their voice and interests are not overshadowed by the majority. It provides a shield against discrimination and ensures inclusivity in governance.
10. Enabling Constitutional Review: Constitutional law

empowers courts to review laws and government actions for their constitutionality. This process of judicial review ensures that legislation and executive actions align with the principles laid down in the constitution.

11. Fostering Social Cohesion: Constitutions often reflect the shared values, history, and aspirations of a nation. They promote social cohesion by providing a sense of identity and purpose, strengthening the bonds among citizens.

In conclusion, constitutional law plays a foundational role in governance, providing the framework for government operations and protecting individual rights and liberties. By upholding the rule of law, limiting government power, and promoting democratic principles, constitutional law fosters a just and accountable society. It empowers citizens to participate in governance, ensures stability, and guides the nation towards progress and prosperity while preserving the core values that define the nation's identity.

Foundational Principles of Constitutional Law

The foundational principles of constitutional law serve as the cornerstones upon which the legal and political systems of a nation are built. These principles are fundamental to the functioning of constitutional democracies and provide the framework for government operations. Here are some of the key foundational principles of constitutional law:

1. The Rule of Law: The rule of law is a fundamental principle that asserts that all individuals, including government officials, are bound by and subject to the law. It ensures that the exercise of governmental authority is based on legal rules and procedures, promoting a society governed by laws rather than by the arbitrary exercise of power.

2. Separation of Powers: The principle of separation of powers divides government authority among three distinct branches: the executive, legislative, and judicial. Each branch has its own functions and responsibilities, acting as a check on the powers of the others to prevent any one branch from becoming too dominant.

3. Federalism: Federalism is a system of government in which power is shared between a central (national) government and subnational entities, such as states or provinces. This principle defines the distribution of powers and responsibilities between the central government and regional or local governments.

4. Judicial Review: Judicial review is the power of the judiciary to review the constitutionality of laws and government actions. This principle ensures that laws and actions by the executive and legislative branches comply with the constitution, and it enables courts to strike down laws that are found to be unconstitutional.

5. Fundamental Rights and Liberties: Constitutional law guarantees fundamental rights and liberties to individuals. These rights, often enshrined in a Bill of Rights or a similar provision, protect citizens from government infringement on their freedoms, such as freedom of speech, religion, and privacy.

6. Popular Sovereignty: Popular sovereignty asserts that the source of governmental authority lies with the people. In a democratic system, the government derives its legitimacy from the consent of the governed, and the people have the right to participate in decision-making through free and fair elections.

7. Constitutional Supremacy: Constitutional supremacy means that the constitution is the highest law of the land, and all laws, including those enacted by the legislature, must conform to its provisions. This principle ensures that the constitution prevails over other legal rules and acts as the ultimate authority in the legal system.

8. Due Process of Law: Due process of law ensures that individuals are treated fairly and justly in legal proceedings. It guarantees that all individuals have the right to be heard, to know the charges against them, and to have access to a fair and impartial judicial process.

9. Equality before the Law: This principle mandates that all individuals are equal in the eyes of the law, regardless of their race, gender, religion, or social status. It prevents discrimination and ensures that all

individuals are entitled to the same legal protections and rights.

10. Supremacy of the Constitution: This principle emphasizes that the constitution is the highest law of the land, and all governmental actions and laws must conform to its provisions. The constitution serves as the supreme legal authority, and any laws or actions inconsistent with it are deemed invalid.

These foundational principles form the basis for a constitutional democracy, ensuring the protection of individual rights, the accountability of government, and the rule of law. They are essential for promoting a just and stable society, empowering citizens, and guiding the course of governance in a nation.

The Rule of Law and its Significance

The Rule of Law is a fundamental principle of constitutional governance that ensures a just and orderly society based on the supremacy of law. It serves as a cornerstone of modern democracies and is essential for upholding individual rights, promoting government accountability, and maintaining social stability. The significance of the Rule of Law lies in its role in shaping the framework for governance and safeguarding the principles of justice, fairness, and equality.

Key Aspects of the Rule of Law:

1. Equality before the Law: The Rule of Law mandates that all individuals, including government officials, are subject to and bound by the law. It ensures that no one is above the law, and all citizens are equal in the eyes of the law, regardless of their social status, wealth, or position.

2. Legal Certainty and Predictability: The Rule of Law provides legal certainty and predictability by establishing clear and accessible laws, rules, and procedures. It allows individuals to understand their rights and obligations and empowers them to seek legal recourse in case of disputes.

3. Limitation of Government Power: One of the essential functions of the Rule of Law is to limit the exercise of government authority. It establishes the boundaries of governmental power, preventing arbitrary actions and safeguarding individual liberties from unwarranted intrusion.

4. Due Process and Fairness: The Rule of Law ensures that

legal proceedings are conducted with due process and fairness. It guarantees that individuals have the right to be heard, know the charges against them, and have access to a fair and impartial judicial process.

5. Judicial Independence: The Rule of Law requires an independent judiciary that can act as a check on the executive and legislative branches. An impartial judiciary ensures that legal decisions are based on law and not influenced by political considerations.

Significance of the Rule of Law:

1. Protection of Individual Rights: The Rule of Law serves as a shield against government actions that violate individual rights and liberties. It provides a legal framework for safeguarding freedom of speech, religion, privacy, and other fundamental rights.

2. Government Accountability: By subjecting government actions to the law, the Rule of Law fosters government accountability. Public officials are held accountable for their decisions and actions, and citizens can challenge government decisions that violate legal norms.

3. Social Stability: The Rule of Law contributes to social stability by providing a predictable and orderly environment. When the law is consistently applied and respected, it reduces the likelihood of social unrest and promotes public confidence in the legal system.

4. Economic Development: The Rule of Law is crucial for economic development and investment. It creates a business-friendly environment, where contracts are enforced, property rights are protected, and legal disputes can be resolved impartially.

5. Upholding Democratic Principles: In a democratic society, the Rule of Law upholds the principles of popular sovereignty and ensures that government

actions are based on the consent of the governed. It prevents the abuse of power and maintains the integrity of democratic institutions.

6. Preservation of Human Dignity: The Rule of Law upholds human dignity by treating all individuals with respect and fairness under the law. It prohibits arbitrary detention, torture, and other forms of human rights violations.

In conclusion, the Rule of Law is a critical foundation for a just and democratic society. Its significance lies in its role in protecting individual rights, promoting government accountability, and maintaining social stability. The Rule of Law is essential for upholding the principles of justice, fairness, and equality, ensuring that all individuals are treated with dignity and respect under the law.

Separation of Powers: Balancing Government Functions

The separation of powers is a fundamental principle of constitutional governance that aims to prevent the concentration of power in any one branch of government. It divides the functions and responsibilities of government among three distinct branches – the executive, legislative, and judicial – and creates a system of checks and balances to ensure accountability and protect individual liberties. The concept of separation of powers was prominently advocated by political philosophers like Montesquieu and is a cornerstone of many modern democracies.

Key Components of the Separation of Powers:

1. Legislative Branch: The legislative branch, typically a parliament or congress, is responsible for making laws. It drafts, debates, and passes legislation that governs society, reflecting the will of the people through elected representatives.
2. Executive Branch: The executive branch, headed by the president, prime minister, or a similar position, is responsible for enforcing and implementing laws. It is tasked with administering government policies and decisions and has the authority to execute laws passed by the legislature.
3. Judicial Branch: The judicial branch, composed of independent courts and judges, is responsible for interpreting laws and ensuring their constitutionality.

It adjudicates disputes, resolves conflicts, and upholds the rule of law by providing impartial and fair judgments.

Significance of the Separation of Powers:

1. Checks and Balances: The separation of powers creates a system of checks and balances, where each branch has the ability to restrain and oversee the actions of the other branches. This system ensures that no single branch becomes too dominant or tyrannical.
2. Accountability: Separating government functions allows for greater accountability. Each branch is accountable to different constituencies, with the legislature accountable to the electorate, the executive accountable to the legislature, and the judiciary accountable to the law and the constitution.
3. Protection of Individual Rights: The separation of powers is a safeguard against potential abuses of government authority that could threaten individual rights and liberties. By dividing power, it limits the potential for oppression and tyranny.
4. Flexibility and Adaptability: The separation of powers allows each branch to focus on its core functions, promoting specialization and expertise. This division of labor enhances efficiency and the ability to adapt to changing circumstances.
5. Independence of the Judiciary: Separating the judiciary from the other branches preserves its independence and impartiality. This independence is essential for upholding the rule of law and ensuring that legal decisions are not influenced by political considerations.
6. Deliberative Process: The separation of powers fosters a deliberative process in lawmaking and governance. The various branches must engage in dialogue,

negotiation, and compromise to achieve their objectives, promoting democratic decision-making.

7. Preservation of Democracy: By distributing power and ensuring checks and balances, the separation of powers preserves the democratic nature of the government. It helps prevent the rise of authoritarianism and promotes the participation of citizens in the governance process.

Overall, the separation of powers is a foundational principle that underpins the functioning of constitutional democracies. By balancing government functions and providing a system of checks and balances, it ensures that government authority is limited, accountable, and directed towards the protection of individual rights and the common good.

Federalism and Distribution of Powers

Federalism is a system of government in which power is divided and shared between a central (national) government and subnational entities, such as states, provinces, or regions. It is a form of governance that allows for a dual system of authority, wherein each level of government retains certain powers and functions while cooperating on matters of mutual interest. The distribution of powers in a federal system is defined by the constitution, which delineates the areas of authority for the central and subnational governments. Federalism is common in many countries, including the United States, Canada, Australia, India, and Germany.

Key Features of Federalism:

1. Division of Powers: In a federal system, the constitution specifies which powers are assigned to the central government and which are reserved for the subnational entities. This division of powers aims to strike a balance between national unity and regional autonomy.
2. Enumerated Powers: The central government possesses specific, enumerated powers listed in the constitution. These powers are typically related to matters of national concern, such as defense, foreign affairs, currency, and international trade.
3. Residual Powers: The subnational entities retain powers not explicitly granted to the central government, known as residual powers. These may include areas like education, health, transportation, and local governance.

4. Concurrent Powers: Some powers are shared by both the central and subnational governments in a federal system. Concurrent powers may include taxation, law enforcement, environmental regulation, and transportation.

5. Supremacy Clause: The constitution in a federal system typically includes a supremacy clause, which establishes that the national constitution and laws passed by the central government are the supreme law of the land, overriding any conflicting laws or regulations at the subnational level.

Significance of Federalism and Distribution of Powers:

1. Balancing Central Authority and Regional Autonomy: Federalism seeks to strike a balance between the need for a strong central authority to address national issues and the desire for regional autonomy to address local concerns. It allows for flexibility in governance while maintaining national unity.

2. Diverse Policy Experimentation: Federal systems enable different subnational entities to adopt diverse policies, laws, and regulations suited to their specific needs and preferences. This allows for experimentation and innovation in governance.

3. Responsive Governance: Federalism brings government closer to the people, as subnational governments can respond more effectively to local demands and concerns. Citizens can influence policies and decisions at both the central and regional levels.

4. Peaceful Resolution of Conflicts: Federal systems can provide a mechanism for peacefully managing and resolving conflicts between different regions or communities within the country. The autonomy granted to subnational entities allows for the accommodation of regional differences and interests.

5. Protection of Minority Rights: Federalism can safeguard the rights and interests of minority communities by granting them significant decision-making power at the subnational level, promoting inclusivity and representation.

6. Economic Development: Federalism can promote economic development by allowing subnational entities to adopt policies and regulations that address specific economic needs and attract investments tailored to local conditions.

7. Stability and Decentralization: Federalism can contribute to political stability by decentralizing power and preventing the concentration of authority in one central government. This reduces the risk of authoritarianism and promotes the participation of diverse regions in governance.

Overall, federalism and the distribution of powers play a crucial role in fostering a cooperative and balanced system of governance. By sharing authority between the central government and subnational entities, federal systems can accommodate regional diversity, promote democratic decision-making, and ensure that government policies and laws reflect the needs and aspirations of the entire nation.

Judicial Review: Ensuring Constitutional Supremacy

Judicial review is a crucial component of constitutional governance, ensuring the supremacy of the constitution and upholding the rule of law. It grants courts the authority to review the constitutionality of laws, regulations, and government actions, and to determine whether they align with the principles and provisions of the constitution. Judicial review is particularly significant in countries with written constitutions, where the constitution is the supreme law of the land and serves as the ultimate authority.

Key Aspects of Judicial Review:

1. Constitutionality Review: Judicial review allows courts to examine the constitutionality of laws and government actions to ensure they do not violate the rights and principles enshrined in the constitution. If a law or action is found to be inconsistent with the constitution, it can be declared unconstitutional and, therefore, void.

2. Protecting Individual Rights: One of the primary purposes of judicial review is to protect individual rights and liberties from potential government encroachment. Courts act as guardians of these rights and provide a forum for individuals to challenge laws or actions that infringe upon their constitutional rights.

3. Safeguarding the Rule of Law: Judicial review

reinforces the principle of the rule of law by subjecting government actions to legal scrutiny. It ensures that all government actions are based on legal authority and that the government is bound by the same laws as its citizens.

4. Balancing Separation of Powers: Judicial review helps maintain the balance of power among the three branches of government by allowing the judiciary to act as a check on the executive and legislative branches. Courts can strike down laws or executive actions that exceed the limits of their constitutional authority.

5. Interpretation of the Constitution: Judicial review involves interpreting the constitution and determining its meaning in specific cases. Courts play a vital role in shaping constitutional law by providing guidance on the application of constitutional principles to modern societal issues.

6. Preserving Democracy: Judicial review safeguards democracy by ensuring that laws and government actions comply with constitutional norms. It prevents the majority from infringing upon the rights of minorities and helps maintain the integrity of democratic institutions.

Significance of Judicial Review:

1. Constitutional Supremacy: Judicial review reinforces the notion of constitutional supremacy, which means that the constitution is the highest law of the land, and all laws and actions must conform to its provisions. It ensures that no branch of government operates beyond the bounds of the constitution.

2. Rule of Law and Government Accountability: Judicial review enhances government accountability by subjecting laws and actions to legal scrutiny. It

promotes transparency and ensures that government officials act within the confines of the law.

3. Protection of Fundamental Rights: Judicial review serves as a vital mechanism for protecting fundamental rights and liberties. It provides a forum for individuals and groups to seek redress when their rights are violated by government actions.

4. Stability and Continuity: Judicial review contributes to stability and continuity in governance by providing consistent interpretations of the constitution. This helps avoid arbitrary changes in laws and policies based on shifting political winds.

5. Social Progress: Through judicial review, courts can influence social progress by striking down discriminatory laws and advancing principles of equality and justice. This allows the law to adapt to changing societal norms and values.

In summary, judicial review plays a crucial role in ensuring constitutional supremacy, protecting individual rights, and upholding the rule of law. By allowing the judiciary to review the constitutionality of laws and government actions, judicial review reinforces democratic governance, maintains the balance of power, and safeguards the rights and liberties of citizens in a constitutional democracy.

Fundamental Rights and Liberties

Fundamental rights and liberties are the basic and inherent rights that every individual possesses by virtue of being human. They are considered essential for human dignity, personal autonomy, and the development of human potential. These rights are often enshrined in constitutions, international treaties, and human rights declarations to protect individuals from abuse and ensure their well-being in diverse societies. The recognition and protection of fundamental rights and liberties are central to the concept of human rights and the principles of justice and equality.

Key Characteristics of Fundamental Rights and Liberties:

1. Universality: Fundamental rights and liberties are universal, applying to all individuals regardless of their nationality, race, religion, gender, or any other status. They are inalienable and cannot be taken away under any circumstances.
2. Inherent and Inviolable: These rights are considered inherent to human beings, meaning they exist simply because individuals are human. They are deemed inviolable and cannot be arbitrarily deprived or violated by governments or other entities.
3. Interdependence and Indivisibility: Fundamental rights and liberties are interdependent and indivisible. The protection of one right often requires the respect and protection of others. For example, the right to freedom of speech may rely on the right to privacy and vice versa.
4. Limitations and Balancing: While fundamental rights

are fundamental, they are not absolute. In some cases, rights may be subject to reasonable limitations, such as restrictions to protect public safety or the rights of others. Courts often engage in balancing exercises to weigh competing rights and interests.

5. Non-Discrimination: Fundamental rights and liberties are granted without discrimination. They apply equally to all individuals, and no one should be denied these rights based on characteristics such as race, gender, religion, or nationality.

Examples of Fundamental Rights and Liberties:

1. Right to Life: The right to life is considered the most fundamental of all rights. It protects individuals from arbitrary deprivation of life and encompasses the prohibition of torture, extrajudicial killings, and unlawful use of force.

2. Freedom of Expression: This right allows individuals to express their opinions, ideas, and beliefs freely without fear of censorship or punishment. It includes freedom of speech, press, assembly, and association.

3. Right to Privacy: The right to privacy protects individuals from unwarranted intrusion into their personal life, communications, and private affairs.

4. Right to Equality: This right ensures that all individuals are equal before the law and are entitled to equal protection and benefit of the law without discrimination.

5. Freedom of Religion: This right grants individuals the freedom to practice their religion or belief of choice and protects against religious discrimination.

6. Right to Due Process: The right to due process guarantees fair and impartial treatment in legal proceedings, including the right to a fair trial, access to legal representation, and the presumption of

innocence.

7. Right to Education: The right to education ensures access to quality education for all individuals, without discrimination, to facilitate the development of their potential and knowledge.
8. Right to Health: The right to health encompasses access to healthcare, sanitation, and medical services to ensure individuals' physical and mental well-being.

These examples represent a selection of fundamental rights and liberties that are commonly recognized and protected by constitutional and international human rights frameworks. The recognition and protection of these rights are essential for fostering a just, free, and democratic society that respects the dignity and worth of every individual.

Drafting and Amending Constitutions

Drafting and amending constitutions are complex processes that involve careful deliberation, negotiation, and consideration of the values and aspirations of a nation. Constitutions serve as the foundational legal documents that establish the structure of government, define the rights and responsibilities of citizens, and set the principles for governance. The process of drafting and amending constitutions varies from country to country, but some common steps and considerations are involved:

Drafting a Constitution:

1. Preparatory Phase: Before the drafting process begins, there is usually a preparatory phase that involves public consultation, expert analysis, and the establishment of a drafting committee or commission. This phase aims to gather input from various stakeholders, including citizens, civil society organizations, and legal experts.
2. Framing the Preamble: The constitution typically starts with a preamble that sets out the purpose, values, and guiding principles of the document. It may express the nation's commitment to democracy, justice, equality, human rights, and the rule of law.
3. Dividing Powers and Structure of Government: The constitution outlines the structure of government, including the division of powers between the executive, legislative, and judicial branches. It may define the roles and functions of each branch and establish a system of checks and balances.
4. Protection of Fundamental Rights: Constitutions

commonly include a bill of rights or a list of fundamental rights and liberties guaranteed to citizens. These rights protect individuals from government infringement and form the core of human rights protection.

5. Designing Electoral Systems: The constitution may detail the electoral system for electing representatives, the qualifications for holding public office, and the procedures for conducting elections.

6. Defining Citizenship and National Identity: The constitution typically addresses issues related to citizenship, including who is considered a citizen and the rights and responsibilities of citizenship.

7. Devolution and Federalism (if applicable): If the country adopts a federal or decentralized system, the constitution may allocate powers between the central government and subnational entities.

8. Constitutional Amendment Process: The drafting process may also include provisions for amending the constitution, specifying the procedures and requirements for making changes to the document in the future.

Amending a Constitution:

1. Proposal for Amendment: Constitutional amendments can be proposed by various entities, including the government, members of the legislature, or through popular initiatives or referendums.

2. Deliberation and Debate: The proposed amendment goes through a process of deliberation and debate within the legislative body or a special constitutional assembly. The proposed amendment may require a supermajority or other specified majority for approval.

3. Public Consultation: In some countries, proposed amendments may be subject to public consultation to

gather input from citizens and stakeholders.

4. Ratification: Once the proposed amendment is approved, it may require ratification by a specified majority of the electorate through a referendum or other mechanisms.

5. Incorporation into the Constitution: If ratified, the amendment is incorporated into the constitution, becoming a part of the supreme law of the land.

It is essential that the process of drafting and amending constitutions be inclusive, transparent, and participatory to reflect the will and interests of the people. Careful consideration should be given to protecting fundamental rights, promoting democratic principles, and ensuring the stability and adaptability of the constitution to meet the evolving needs of society.

Constituent Assembly and Constitutional Drafting

A Constituent Assembly is a representative body or committee specifically tasked with the responsibility of drafting and adopting a new constitution or amending an existing one. It is a critical phase in the process of constitution-making and plays a vital role in shaping the legal and political foundation of a nation. Constituent Assemblies are often established during periods of significant political change, such as after a revolution, independence, or major constitutional reform.

Key Aspects of a Constituent Assembly and Constitutional Drafting:

1. Representative Body: The Constituent Assembly is composed of representatives elected by the people or appointed by other bodies, reflecting the diversity and interests of the population. It is crucial to ensure the inclusive and broad-based representation of various social, political, ethnic, and religious groups.

2. Drafting a New Constitution: In cases where a nation lacks a written constitution, the Constituent Assembly is responsible for drafting an entirely new constitution. This process involves careful deliberation, negotiation, and the crafting of provisions that define the structure of government, protect fundamental rights, and set the principles of governance.

3. Amending an Existing Constitution: In countries with

established constitutions, the Constituent Assembly may be convened to amend or revise the existing constitution to address evolving needs, challenges, or aspirations of the nation. This process may involve partial or comprehensive changes to the existing document.

4. Public Consultation and Participation: A key feature of the Constituent Assembly process is public consultation and participation. The Assembly typically seeks input from citizens, civil society organizations, experts, and other stakeholders through public hearings, surveys, and written submissions to gather diverse perspectives.

5. Preamble and Guiding Principles: Constituent Assemblies often begin the drafting process by framing a preamble that sets out the fundamental values, ideals, and aspirations of the nation. The preamble serves as a guiding statement that informs the rest of the constitution.

6. Fundamental Rights and Liberties: One of the primary tasks of the Constituent Assembly is to enshrine and protect fundamental rights and liberties in the constitution. These rights are considered essential for safeguarding human dignity and ensuring individual freedoms.

7. Division of Powers: The Constituent Assembly establishes the division of powers between the executive, legislative, and judicial branches of government. It defines the roles and responsibilities of each branch to create a system of checks and balances.

8. Federalism and Devolution: If the nation adopts a federal or decentralized system of government, the Constituent Assembly allocates powers between the central government and subnational entities.

9. Electoral Systems and Political Processes: The Assembly may define the electoral system and the

processes for electing representatives, political parties, and public officials.

10. Transparency and Accountability: The Constituent Assembly process should be transparent, with public access to information and decisions, to ensure accountability to the people.

11. Approval and Ratification: Once the constitution is drafted, it must be approved and ratified by the Assembly or through a referendum, depending on the constitutional process.

The successful functioning of a Constituent Assembly depends on effective leadership, cooperation among diverse stakeholders, and a commitment to democratic principles. The process of constitutional drafting should be inclusive, participatory, and aimed at building a constitution that reflects the values and aspirations of the nation while promoting stability, justice, and democratic governance.

Principles of Constitutional Interpretation

Constitutional interpretation is the process by which courts and other governmental bodies interpret the provisions of a constitution to determine their meaning and application to specific cases or situations. The principles of constitutional interpretation guide judges and legal scholars in their analysis of constitutional provisions, ensuring consistent and objective decisions. Different countries may have specific approaches to constitutional interpretation, but some common principles include:

1. Original Intent: This principle seeks to discern and apply the original intent of the framers of the constitution. It involves examining historical documents, debates, and context to understand the framers' intentions when drafting specific provisions.
2. Textualism or Literalism: Textualism emphasizes interpreting the constitution based solely on the plain meaning of the text. Judges give weight to the language used in the constitution without considering external factors or intentions.
3. Purposive Approach: The purposive approach focuses on the underlying purpose or spirit of the constitution. Judges interpret provisions to achieve the broader objectives and principles set out in the constitution, even if the specific language is not explicit.
4. Living Constitution: This approach considers the constitution as a living, evolving document that must adapt to changing times and circumstances. Judges

interpret the constitution in light of contemporary values and societal developments.

5. Precedent (Stare Decisis): Courts often rely on past decisions and established case law to interpret constitutional provisions consistently over time. This principle, known as stare decisis, promotes stability and predictability in constitutional interpretation.

6. Strict Construction: Under this principle, courts interpret the constitution narrowly, limiting the scope of government authority and preferring individual rights over governmental actions.

7. Broad Construction: In contrast, broad construction involves interpreting the constitution expansively to grant the government broader powers or to protect public interests.

8. Avoidance Doctrine: Courts may avoid interpreting constitutional issues when other grounds for decision are available, especially when dealing with controversial or politically sensitive matters.

9. Contextual Analysis: This principle involves considering the broader context in which constitutional provisions are applied, including historical, social, and cultural factors.

10. Balancing of Interests: In cases where constitutional provisions conflict or overlap, courts engage in a balancing exercise, weighing competing interests to find a reasonable resolution.

11. Human Rights Approach: Some countries adopt a human rights approach, giving particular weight to international human rights treaties and principles when interpreting constitutional provisions.

12. National Identity: In nations with a strong sense of national identity, courts may interpret the constitution with reference to the country's historical traditions and values.

13. Preeminence of the Constitution: This principle

emphasizes that the constitution is the supreme law of the land, and all other laws and actions must conform to its provisions.

The choice of interpretive principles can significantly impact the outcome of constitutional cases and influence the development of constitutional law. Judges and legal scholars consider these principles carefully to ensure the consistent and principled application of the constitution to the complexities of contemporary legal and social issues.

Constitutional Amendments: Procedures and Limitations

Constitutional amendments are the formal changes or additions made to a country's constitution. These amendments are crucial for adapting the constitution to changing times, addressing societal needs, and rectifying any deficiencies in the original document. However, the process of amending a constitution is typically more rigorous than that of ordinary legislation, as it involves altering the fundamental law of the land. The procedures and limitations for constitutional amendments vary from country to country, but some common elements include:

1. Amendment Procedures:

a. Proposal: The first step in the amendment process is the proposal of the amendment. The proposal can originate from different sources, such as the legislature, a constituent assembly, a special commission, or through a citizen-led initiative.

b. Approval: Once proposed, the amendment must go through an approval process. This step varies depending on the constitutional framework of the country and may require a specific majority vote in the legislature or a referendum.

c. Ratification: In many countries, after approval by the relevant body, the amendment must be ratified by a specified majority of the electorate through a referendum. This ensures that the amendment has broad public support before becoming part of the constitution.

2. Special Majority Requirement: Many countries require

a special majority vote for the approval and ratification of constitutional amendments. This means that the amendment must secure a higher percentage of votes than typical legislation. Common special majority requirements include a two-thirds majority or three-fourths majority.

3. Entrenchment Clauses: Some constitutions contain "entrenchment clauses" that make certain provisions more difficult to amend. These clauses may require a higher majority or additional procedural steps for specific constitutional provisions.

4. Bill of Rights and Unamendable Provisions: Some countries designate certain provisions, such as the bill of rights or core democratic principles, as "unamendable." These provisions cannot be changed or amended under any circumstances, ensuring the preservation of fundamental rights and democratic principles.

5. Time Limitations: In some countries, there may be time limitations between the proposal, approval, and ratification stages to prevent hasty decision-making and allow for public debate and consultation.

6. Regional or Subnational Approval: In federal systems or countries with regional autonomy, constitutional amendments may require approval from regional or subnational entities.

7. Judicial Review: Courts in some countries have the authority to review the constitutionality of proposed amendments to ensure they do not violate other provisions of the constitution or fundamental principles.

8. Consensus-Building: Constitutional amendments often require consensus-building among different political parties, stakeholders, and societal groups. This fosters inclusivity and ensures broad-based support for the proposed changes.

9. Constitutional Convention: In some countries, constitutional amendments are proposed and approved through a constitutional convention, where elected representatives or delegates gather to draft and amend the constitution.

Limitations on Constitutional Amendments:

1. Fundamental Rights and Democratic Principles: Many constitutions place limitations on amendments that would undermine the fundamental rights of citizens or the core principles of democracy, such as the rule of law and separation of powers.
2. Unamendable Clauses: As mentioned earlier, some constitutions designate certain provisions as unamendable, protecting essential aspects of the constitution from alteration.
3. Amendment Limits: Some constitutions may set limits on the number of amendments that can be proposed within a specific time frame to prevent frequent and disruptive changes to the constitution.
4. Protecting Minority Rights: Constitutional amendments should not infringe upon the rights and interests of minority groups or lead to the marginalization of particular communities.
5. Protecting Federal Structure: In federal systems, amendments should respect the balance of power between the central government and subnational entities.
6. Public Participation: Limitations may require that constitutional amendments be subject to public consultation or referendums to ensure democratic legitimacy.

The process of amending a constitution is intentionally challenging to prevent hasty and ill-considered changes to the fundamental law of the country. The procedures and limitations are designed to strike a balance between the need for flexibility and the preservation of the constitution's foundational principles and values.

Constitutional Institutions and Their Functions

Constitutional institutions are key components of a country's governance system, established and empowered by the constitution to fulfill specific functions in the administration of the state and the protection of citizens' rights. These institutions play a vital role in upholding the rule of law, ensuring accountability, and safeguarding democratic principles. The specific constitutional institutions and their functions may vary depending on the country's political system and the provisions of its constitution. However, some common constitutional institutions and their functions include:

1. Executive Branch:

Function: The executive branch is responsible for implementing and enforcing laws, managing the day-to-day affairs of the government, and representing the country on the international stage.

Key Institutions:

- President: The head of state and government in presidential systems.
- Prime Minister: The head of government in parliamentary systems.
- Cabinet: A group of ministers appointed by the head of government to oversee specific government departments.
2. Legislative Branch:

Function: The legislative branch is responsible for making and enacting laws, representing the interests of the people, and overseeing the actions of the executive branch.

Key Institutions:

- Parliament or Congress: The primary legislative body, consisting of elected representatives or members of parliament.
- Senate: In bicameral systems, the upper house of the legislature, often representing regional or state interests.
- House of Representatives or Lower House: The lower chamber of the legislature, representing the population directly.

3. Judicial Branch:

Function: The judicial branch is responsible for interpreting laws, ensuring their constitutionality, resolving disputes, and upholding justice.

Key Institutions:

- Supreme Court: The highest court in the country, responsible for interpreting the constitution and making final decisions on legal matters.
- Constitutional Court: In some countries, a specialized court dedicated to reviewing the constitutionality of laws and government actions.
- Lower Courts: Various levels of courts that handle civil, criminal, and administrative cases.

4. Independent Commissions and Agencies:

Function: These institutions are responsible for overseeing specific areas of public interest and ensuring impartiality and fairness in their respective domains.

Key Institutions:

- Election Commission: Responsible for organizing and conducting elections, ensuring their integrity and fairness.
- Human Rights Commission: Charged with protecting and promoting human rights within the country.
- Anti-Corruption Commission: Tasked with investigating and combating corruption in public institutions.

5. Central Bank:

Function: The central bank is responsible for managing the country's monetary policy, currency, and financial stability.

Key Institution:

- Central Bank: An independent institution that controls the money supply, interest rates, and exchange rates, aiming to achieve stable economic growth and price stability.

6. Ombudsman:

Function: The ombudsman is an independent office responsible for investigating complaints of maladministration and government misconduct.

7. Auditor-General:

Function: The Auditor-General oversees and audits government expenditures to ensure transparency and accountability in the use of public funds.

These constitutional institutions work together to ensure the effective functioning of the state, the protection of citizens' rights, and the promotion of good governance. The separation of powers and checks and balances among these institutions play a crucial role in preventing the concentration of power and safeguarding democracy.

Executive Branch: Presidential vs. Parliamentary Systems

Presidential and parliamentary systems are two distinct forms of executive governance found in democratic countries. They differ in how the executive branch is structured, the role of the head of state and government, the relationship between the executive and legislative branches, and the process of leadership selection. Here's a comparison of the two systems:

Presidential System:

1. Executive Structure: In a presidential system, the executive branch is separate from the legislative branch. The president, as the head of state and government, holds executive authority independently of the legislature.
2. Head of State and Government: The president serves as both the head of state and the head of government. They are directly elected by the people in a national election or an electoral college system.
3. Executive Powers: The president wields significant executive powers, including the authority to appoint and dismiss government officials, propose budgets, implement policies, and serve as the commander-in-chief of the armed forces.
4. Legislative Relationship: In a presidential system, the president and the legislature are independent of each other. The president cannot dissolve the legislature, and the legislature cannot remove the president

through a vote of no confidence.

5. Separation of Powers: The separation of powers between the executive and legislative branches is a defining feature of the presidential system. Each branch operates independently, providing a system of checks and balances.

Examples of Countries with Presidential Systems: United States, Brazil, Mexico.

Parliamentary System:

1. Executive Structure: In a parliamentary system, the executive branch is integrated with the legislative branch. The head of government is typically the leader of the majority party or coalition in the parliament.

2. Head of State and Government: The head of state is a ceremonial figurehead, often a monarch or a president with limited powers. The head of government, known as the prime minister, is the chief executive and is usually the leader of the majority party in the parliament.

3. Executive Powers: The prime minister holds executive authority, but their powers are constrained by the parliament. They are accountable to the parliament and can be removed through a vote of no confidence.

4. Legislative Relationship: The executive branch is dependent on the confidence of the parliament. The government's policies and decisions must have the support of the majority in the parliament to stay in power.

5. Fusion of Powers: In a parliamentary system, there is a fusion of powers between the executive and legislative branches. The government is formed from the majority party or coalition in the parliament, leading to a closer relationship between the two branches.

Examples of Countries with Parliamentary Systems: United Kingdom, Canada, Germany.

Key Differences Summarized:

Presidential System:

- Separation of powers between the executive and legislative branches.
- Directly elected president as the head of state and government.
- President holds significant executive powers independently.
- No vote of no confidence to remove the president.
- Limited interaction between the president and the legislature.

Parliamentary System:

- Fusion of powers between the executive and legislative branches.
- Head of state is ceremonial; head of government is the prime minister.
- Prime minister's powers are subject to parliament's confidence.
- Prime minister can be removed through a vote of no confidence.
- Close interaction between the executive and the legislature.

Legislative Branch: Bicameralism and Lawmaking

Bicameralism is a system of legislative organization in which the legislative branch of government consists of two separate chambers or houses. These chambers typically have distinct functions and powers, and they work together to make and enact laws. Bicameral legislatures are common in many democratic countries and are believed to offer certain advantages, such as promoting checks and balances and providing a forum for diverse representation. Let's explore the legislative branch's functions in a bicameral system and the process of lawmaking:

Functions of the Legislative Branch in a Bicameral System:

1. Lawmaking: The primary function of the legislative branch is to make and enact laws. Both chambers participate in the lawmaking process, considering proposed legislation and deciding whether to approve, amend, or reject it.
2. Representation: Bicameral legislatures offer a broader representation of the people's interests and views. The two chambers may have different methods of representation, such as one based on population size (House of Representatives) and another providing equal representation for all regions (Senate).
3. Checks and Balances: Bicameralism contributes to the system of checks and balances by ensuring that proposed legislation is subject to scrutiny by both

chambers. Each chamber can act as a check on the other's actions, helping to prevent the concentration of power in one branch.

4. Review and Oversight: Both chambers have the authority to review and oversee the actions of the executive branch. They can summon government officials for questioning, investigate issues of public concern, and scrutinize government activities.

5. Approval of Budgets: The legislative branch is responsible for approving government budgets and financial expenditures. This ensures that public funds are allocated and spent in accordance with the law and public interest.

6. Confirmation of Appointments: In some systems, the upper chamber (often the Senate) has the power to confirm or reject appointments made by the executive, such as cabinet members, judges, and ambassadors.

Process of Lawmaking in a Bicameral System:

1. Bill Introduction: The legislative process begins when a member of either chamber introduces a proposed law, known as a bill. The bill can address various issues, such as social policies, taxation, or infrastructure.

2. Committee Consideration: The bill is referred to relevant committees in both chambers for in-depth examination and analysis. Committees review the bill's content, hold hearings to gather input from experts and stakeholders, and may suggest amendments.

3. Floor Debate and Voting: After committee consideration, the bill proceeds to the floor of each chamber for debate. Lawmakers can propose amendments and discuss the bill's merits before voting on its passage.

4. Reconciliation: If the two chambers pass different versions of the same bill, a process of reconciliation may occur to resolve the differences. A conference committee, consisting of members from both chambers, works to create a unified version of the bill.

5. Final Approval: Once the bill is agreed upon by both chambers, it is sent to the head of state (usually the president or monarch) for approval. Depending on the country's constitutional provisions, the head of state may have the power to veto the bill, send it back for further consideration, or sign it into law.

6. Enactment: If the bill receives the head of state's approval, it becomes law and is officially enacted. It will be published and integrated into the legal framework, with provisions on implementation and enforcement.

Bicameral legislatures offer a forum for robust debate, representation, and consensus-building, contributing to the functioning and stability of democratic systems. By involving two chambers in the lawmaking process, bicameralism promotes careful consideration of legislation and fosters a greater range of perspectives and ideas.

Judiciary: Structure, Independence, and Judicial Activism

The judiciary is a vital component of the state's governance structure, responsible for interpreting and applying the law, resolving disputes, and upholding justice. Its independence is crucial to ensure impartiality and fairness in legal proceedings and to serve as a check on the executive and legislative branches of government. The concept of judicial activism relates to the role of the judiciary in actively shaping public policy and interpreting the constitution in a more expansive and interventionist manner. Let's explore the structure, independence, and concept of judicial activism:

1. Structure of the Judiciary:

The structure of the judiciary can vary from country to country, but it typically consists of multiple levels or tiers. Common elements include:

a. Lower Courts: The judiciary often includes lower courts, such as district courts or magistrate courts, which handle civil and criminal cases at the local level.

b. Appellate Courts: Above the lower courts are intermediate appellate courts, where parties dissatisfied with lower court decisions can appeal for review.

c. Supreme Court: The highest court in the judiciary, responsible for reviewing important legal issues, constitutional matters, and cases of national significance.

2. Judicial Independence:

Judicial independence refers to the judiciary's ability to make decisions without external interference, pressure, or influence from the other branches of government or powerful entities. Key elements of judicial independence include:

a. Tenure and Removal: Judges often have secure and fixed terms of office to protect them from arbitrary removal, ensuring that they can make decisions based on the law without fear of repercussions.

b. Financial Autonomy: The judiciary should have adequate funding and control over its budget to function independently without reliance on other branches of government for financial support.

c. Non-Interference: The judiciary should be free from interference by the executive or legislative branches and not be subject to political influence.

d. Rule of Law: Judicial independence is closely linked to the rule of law, ensuring that all individuals, including government officials, are subject to the law and its equal application.

3. Judicial Activism:

Judicial activism is a concept used to describe a judiciary's willingness to take an active role in shaping public policy and constitutional interpretation. Key features of judicial activism include:

a. Expansive Interpretation: Activist courts may interpret laws and constitutional provisions broadly to address contemporary issues and societal challenges beyond the scope of traditional interpretations.

b. Intervening in Policy Matters: Activist courts may be more willing to intervene in matters of public policy, making decisions that may be traditionally left to the legislative or executive branches.

c. Protecting Rights: Judicial activism can involve an active defense of fundamental rights and liberties, ensuring their protection even in the face of opposition from other branches of government.

d. Impact on Social Change: Activist courts' decisions may have a significant impact on social change and legal developments in a country.

It is important to note that the concept of judicial activism can be controversial and is often viewed differently by various legal and political perspectives. Some see it as essential for protecting rights and promoting justice, while others argue that it can lead to judicial overreach and undermine the democratic process.

In democratic societies, maintaining an independent and impartial judiciary is crucial for upholding the rule of law, safeguarding individual rights, and ensuring a fair and just legal system. The balance between judicial independence and judicial restraint, along with the concept of judicial activism, remains an ongoing debate in constitutional law and governance.

Role of Constitutional Courts in Protecting Rights

Constitutional courts play a crucial role in protecting rights and upholding the rule of law within a democratic system. Their primary function is to interpret and apply the constitution, including its provisions related to fundamental rights and liberties. As independent and specialized institutions, constitutional courts have the authority to review the constitutionality of laws, government actions, and policies to ensure they align with the constitution's principles. Here are the key ways in which constitutional courts protect rights:

1. Constitutional Review:

One of the central functions of constitutional courts is to engage in constitutional review, which involves assessing the constitutionality of laws, executive orders, and administrative decisions. When a law or action is challenged before the constitutional court, the court examines whether it conforms to the rights and principles enshrined in the constitution. If it is found to be unconstitutional, the court may strike down the law or action, rendering it null and void.

2. Safeguarding Fundamental Rights:

Constitutional courts safeguard fundamental rights and liberties by ensuring that legislation and government actions respect these rights. They act as a powerful check against potential abuses of power and violations of citizens' rights by the government.

3. Balancing Rights:

Constitutional courts often face cases in which different rights are in conflict with each other or with other public interests. They play a critical role in striking a balance between competing rights and interests to protect individual liberties while also considering broader societal concerns.

4. Judicial Enforcement:

Constitutional courts have the authority to enforce their decisions, ensuring that their rulings are respected and implemented. Their judgments are binding on all branches of government, including the executive and legislative branches, as well as other public authorities.

5. Review of Human Rights Violations:

Constitutional courts may review cases of alleged human rights violations, providing an avenue for individuals to seek justice when their rights have been infringed upon.

6. Providing Legal Clarity:

By interpreting constitutional provisions related to rights, constitutional courts provide legal clarity and guidance to lawmakers, government agencies, and citizens, helping to avoid ambiguity and ensuring consistent application of the law.

7. Public Education:

Constitutional courts also have an educational role, raising public awareness about constitutional rights and their significance in protecting individual freedoms and promoting a just society.

8. Acting as a Bulwark Against Abuse of Power:

Through their independence and impartiality, constitutional courts act as a bulwark against potential abuses of power by other branches of government. They ensure that all government actions are subject to scrutiny and adhere to the principles set forth in the constitution.

Overall, constitutional courts serve as guardians of the constitution and its values, playing a critical role in upholding fundamental rights, promoting the rule of law, and maintaining the democratic principles of a nation. Their commitment to justice and fairness helps preserve the balance of power and protects the rights and liberties of citizens.

Constitutional Principles in Practice: Case Studies

Case Study 1: Brown v. Board of Education (1954) - United States

In Brown v. Board of Education, the United States Supreme Court addressed the issue of racial segregation in public schools. The case involved several lawsuits challenging the constitutionality of racially segregated schools, where African American children were forced to attend separate schools from white children. The plaintiffs argued that segregated schools violated the Equal Protection Clause of the Fourteenth Amendment to the U.S. Constitution, which guarantees equal treatment under the law.

The Supreme Court, in a unanimous decision, held that racial segregation in public education was inherently unequal and violated the Equal Protection Clause. Chief Justice Earl Warren famously wrote, "In the field of public education, the doctrine of 'separate but equal' has no place. Separate educational facilities are inherently unequal." This landmark decision effectively ended legal segregation in public schools and paved the way for the desegregation of other public facilities and institutions.

Case Study 2: Kesavananda Bharati v. State of Kerala (1973) - India

Kesavananda Bharati v. State of Kerala was a landmark case in Indian constitutional history that dealt with the extent of Parliament's power to amend the Indian Constitution. The case arose from a dispute regarding the constitutionality of the Twenty-Fourth Amendment Act, which sought to limit the scope of judicial review.

The Supreme Court of India, in a landmark judgment, established the doctrine of "basic structure." The court held that while the Parliament had the power to amend the Constitution, it could not alter its "basic structure," which included features such as the supremacy of the Constitution, the rule of law, fundamental rights, and the democratic and federal character of the Indian state.

This decision ensured that certain core principles and fundamental rights enshrined in the Indian Constitution would be protected from arbitrary amendments, safeguarding the essence of India's democratic and constitutional framework.

Case Study 3: Maneka Gandhi v. Union of India (1978) - India

In Maneka Gandhi v. Union of India, the Indian Supreme Court addressed the issue of the right to travel under Article 21 of the Indian Constitution, which guarantees the right to life and personal liberty. Maneka Gandhi's passport had been impounded by the government without providing her an opportunity to be heard, based on a law that allowed the government to do so in the interest of the general public.

The Supreme Court held that the right to travel was an essential part of personal liberty and that any restriction on this right must be fair and reasonable. The court emphasized that the principles of natural justice, which include the right to be heard, must be followed in any situation where a person's fundamental rights might be affected.

This case significantly expanded the scope of Article 21 as an expansive and essential right, ensuring that government actions affecting personal liberty would be subject to scrutiny and fair procedures.

These case studies demonstrate how constitutional principles are put into practice by courts, shaping legal decisions and safeguarding fundamental rights. Constitutional principles provide a framework for addressing complex societal issues and ensuring that government actions and laws align with the core values and principles enshrined in the constitution. Through landmark decisions like those highlighted above, constitutional principles continue to evolve and shape the course of law and governance in various democratic nations.

Freedom of Speech and Expression: Balancing Rights and Responsibilities

Freedom of speech and expression is a fundamental human right that plays a crucial role in promoting democratic values, enabling open debate, and facilitating the exchange of ideas. However, like many rights, it is not an absolute freedom and must be balanced with certain responsibilities to prevent harm and ensure a harmonious society. Striking this balance between individual liberties and societal interests is a complex and ongoing challenge. Here are some key aspects to consider in balancing freedom of speech and expression with responsibilities:

1. Protecting Free Speech:
   - Robust Public Discourse: Freedom of speech fosters a vibrant marketplace of ideas, where individuals can express their opinions, share knowledge, and engage in open debate. This diversity of voices enriches public discourse and democratic decision-making.
   - Political Participation: Freedom of expression empowers citizens to participate in the political process, voice their grievances, and hold governments accountable.
   - Media Freedom: A free press is vital for providing objective information, investigating corruption, and serving as a watchdog on those in power.
2. Balancing Rights and Responsibilities:
   - Harm Principle: One of the key principles in balancing free speech is the harm principle, which suggests that

limitations on speech are justified when it poses a direct threat of harm to individuals or society.

- Hate Speech: While freedom of speech protects diverse opinions, speech that incites hatred, violence, or discrimination against certain groups must be restricted to prevent harm to vulnerable communities.
- Defamation and Privacy: Balancing free speech with the right to privacy and protection from defamation requires thoughtful consideration of how speech can affect individuals' reputations and personal lives.

3. Legal Frameworks:

- Clear and Precise Laws: Legislation should clearly define the limitations on speech to avoid arbitrary or excessive restrictions.
- Independent Judiciary: A robust and impartial judiciary is essential in interpreting and applying the law to ensure consistent and fair decisions on free speech cases.

4. Responsible Journalism and Media:

- Media Ethics: Journalists and media organizations should adhere to ethical standards, fact-checking, and accurate reporting to prevent the dissemination of false information.
- Sensitivity to Vulnerable Groups: Media outlets should be aware of their impact on vulnerable groups and exercise caution in reporting to avoid reinforcing harmful stereotypes.

5. Education and Media Literacy:

- Promoting Media Literacy: Educating the public on critical thinking and media literacy helps individuals discern between reliable information and misinformation or propaganda.
- Responsible Use of Social Media: Encouraging responsible digital citizenship can help reduce the spread of harmful content and promote constructive online communication.

6. Limitations on Government Intervention:
   - Avoiding Censorship: Governments must be cautious not to suppress dissenting voices or manipulate information to maintain power.
   - Proportionality: Any restrictions on free speech should be proportionate to the potential harm and carefully balanced with the broader public interest.

Balancing freedom of speech and expression with responsibilities requires a nuanced approach that considers the evolving societal context, individual rights, and the potential consequences of speech. An open and inclusive dialogue among stakeholders, including governments, civil society, media, and citizens, is essential in navigating these complexities and fostering a society that values both freedom and responsibility.

Right to Privacy and Surveillance in the Digital Age

In the digital age, the right to privacy faces significant challenges due to the rapid advancement of technology and the widespread collection, storage, and analysis of personal data. Digital communication platforms, internet-connected devices, and data-driven technologies have transformed how information is generated, shared, and accessed. As a result, concerns about surveillance and its impact on individuals' right to privacy have become increasingly prominent. Here are some key aspects to consider regarding the right to privacy and surveillance in the digital age:

1. Definition of Right to Privacy:

The right to privacy is a fundamental human right recognized by international human rights law. It encompasses the right to be free from unwarranted intrusion into one's personal life, the right to control and protect one's personal data, and the right to maintain personal autonomy and dignity.

2. Types of Surveillance:
- Government Surveillance: Governments, law enforcement agencies, and intelligence services may use various technologies to monitor individuals, communications, and online activities in the name of national security or public safety.
- Corporate Surveillance: Companies collect vast amounts of data on individuals for various purposes, such as targeted advertising, personalization of

services, and market research.
- Mass Surveillance: Mass surveillance involves the systematic monitoring and analysis of communications and data on a large scale, often without specific suspicion of wrongdoing.

3. Impact on Privacy:
- Data Collection: The constant collection of personal data, often without individuals' awareness or consent, raises concerns about the potential misuse of such information.
- Profiling and Targeting: Surveillance technologies can create detailed profiles of individuals based on their online behavior, leading to personalized advertising and content, but also possible discrimination and manipulation.
- Chilling Effect: Fear of surveillance can stifle free expression and self-censorship, as individuals may become hesitant to share certain thoughts or opinions online.

4. Privacy Laws and Regulations:
- Data Protection: Many countries have data protection laws that regulate the collection, use, and storage of personal data, aiming to protect individuals' privacy.
- Privacy by Design: The concept of privacy by design encourages organizations to build privacy safeguards into their products and services from the outset.

5. Government Surveillance and Human Rights:
- Proportionality: Any government surveillance measures should be necessary and proportionate to achieve legitimate objectives, such as national security or public safety.
- Judicial Oversight: Independent judicial oversight of surveillance activities can help ensure accountability and protect against abuse of power.

6. Technological Solutions:
- Encryption: Encryption technologies can enhance

the security and privacy of digital communications, making it more challenging for unauthorized access.

- Anonymity Tools: Anonymity tools and techniques can allow individuals to browse the internet and communicate online without revealing their identities.

Balancing the need for security and public safety with the protection of individual privacy rights is a complex challenge in the digital age. It requires a thoughtful and comprehensive approach that considers legal, technological, and ethical dimensions. Respecting the right to privacy and establishing responsible surveillance practices are crucial to fostering trust and maintaining a healthy digital society that values both security and individual freedoms.

Equality and Non-Discrimination: Addressing Social Injustices

Equality and non-discrimination are fundamental principles of human rights and social justice. They seek to ensure that all individuals are treated fairly and equally, regardless of their race, ethnicity, gender, religion, disability, or any other characteristic. Addressing social injustices and promoting equality involves challenging and dismantling systems and structures that perpetuate discrimination and marginalization. Here are key aspects to consider in the context of equality and non-discrimination:

1. Understanding Social Injustices:
   - Systemic Discrimination: Social injustices often result from deeply ingrained discriminatory practices and biases that are embedded in social, political, and economic systems.
   - Intersectionality: The concept of intersectionality recognizes that individuals may experience multiple forms of discrimination and marginalization based on the intersection of their identities.
2. Legal Protections and Human Rights:
   - Anti-Discrimination Laws: Many countries have enacted laws that prohibit discrimination and promote equality in various spheres of life, such as employment, education, and housing.
   - International Human Rights Framework: International human rights instruments, such as the Universal Declaration of Human Rights and

the Convention on the Elimination of All Forms of Discrimination Against Women (CEDAW), provide a foundation for addressing discrimination and promoting equality globally.

3. Promoting Inclusive Policies:
- Affirmative Action: In certain contexts, affirmative action policies may be implemented to address historical injustices and provide opportunities to underrepresented or disadvantaged groups.
- Inclusive Education: Ensuring inclusive education systems can promote equal access to quality education for all children, regardless of their background or abilities.

4. Combating Discrimination in Employment:
- Pay Equity: Taking measures to close the gender pay gap and ensure equal pay for equal work is critical to combat gender-based discrimination in the workplace.
- Diversity and Inclusion: Employers can foster diverse and inclusive workplaces by promoting diversity hiring practices and creating an environment that values employees' unique perspectives and backgrounds.

5. Addressing Racial and Ethnic Discrimination:
- Racial Justice: Combating racial discrimination requires acknowledging historical injustices and implementing policies that address systemic racism.
- Minority Rights: Ensuring the protection of minority rights and promoting their participation in decision-making processes can help prevent discrimination against marginalized groups.

6. Combatting Gender Discrimination:
- Gender Equality: Advancing gender equality involves challenging traditional gender roles and stereotypes that perpetuate discrimination and inequality.
- Ending Violence Against Women: Addressing violence against women and girls is essential to achieving

gender equality and promoting a society free from gender-based discrimination.

7. Empowering Marginalized Communities:

- Empowerment Programs: Providing access to education, training, and economic opportunities can empower marginalized communities and promote social inclusion.
- Amplifying Voices: Encouraging representation and participation of marginalized groups in political and public life can amplify their voices and influence policies.

8. Public Awareness and Education:

- Education Campaigns: Public awareness campaigns can challenge stereotypes, raise awareness about discrimination, and foster empathy and understanding.
- Inclusive Curriculum: Incorporating diverse perspectives and histories into educational curricula can promote tolerance and inclusivity from a young age.

Promoting equality and combating discrimination require a collective effort from individuals, communities, civil society organizations, governments, and international bodies. It involves continuous reflection on societal norms, biases, and practices that perpetuate discrimination, and a commitment to building a more just and equitable world for all. By upholding the principles of equality and non-discrimination, we can create a more inclusive and compassionate society that respects the dignity and rights of every individual.

Right to Education and Access to Healthcare Services

The right to education and access to healthcare services are fundamental human rights recognized by various international human rights instruments. These rights are crucial for ensuring the well-being and development of individuals and promoting equitable societies. Let's explore each right and its significance:

Right to Education:

1. Universal Access: The right to education emphasizes that education should be accessible to all individuals, without discrimination. It includes access to primary, secondary, and higher education, as well as vocational and adult education.
2. Quality Education: The right to education not only emphasizes access but also underscores the importance of providing quality education that equips individuals with the knowledge, skills, and capabilities to lead fulfilling lives and contribute to society.
3. Eliminating Barriers: Ensuring the right to education involves eliminating barriers that prevent marginalized groups, such as girls, children with disabilities, and those from disadvantaged backgrounds, from accessing and benefiting from education.
4. Inclusive Education: Inclusive education promotes an education system that accommodates diverse needs and abilities, ensuring that every learner receives

appropriate support and opportunities for learning and growth.

5. Empowerment: Education empowers individuals by providing them with knowledge, critical thinking skills, and the ability to participate in decision-making processes, fostering active and informed citizenship.

6. Economic Development: Access to education is closely linked to a country's economic development. A well-educated workforce can drive innovation, productivity, and economic growth.

Right to Access Healthcare Services:

1. Availability: The right to access healthcare services implies that essential healthcare facilities, goods, and services should be available to all without discrimination.

2. Affordability: Healthcare should be affordable and not result in financial hardship for individuals seeking medical treatment or services.

3. Quality of Care: The right to healthcare includes the provision of quality medical care that is based on scientific evidence and respects patients' dignity and autonomy.

4. Non-Discrimination: Access to healthcare services should be provided without discrimination based on factors such as race, ethnicity, gender, religion, or socio-economic status.

5. Vulnerable Populations: Ensuring the right to healthcare involves paying particular attention to the needs of vulnerable populations, such as children, the elderly, people with disabilities, and those living in poverty.

6. Preventative Care: The right to healthcare also includes access to preventative measures and health promotion programs aimed at preventing diseases and promoting

well-being.
7. Universal Health Coverage: Universal health coverage is a key goal in ensuring the right to access healthcare services, aiming to provide healthcare to all individuals without financial hardship.
8. Public Health: The right to healthcare includes the protection and promotion of public health, including disease prevention, health education, and response to health emergencies.

Both the right to education and the right to access healthcare services are critical for promoting social justice, reducing inequalities, and fostering human development. Governments, civil society organizations, and international bodies play a significant role in ensuring that these rights are upheld and respected, and that necessary resources are allocated to provide quality education and healthcare services to all individuals, regardless of their background or circumstances. By safeguarding and promoting these rights, societies can work towards creating a more equitable and inclusive world that values the well-being and potential of every individual.

Environmental Protection and Sustainable Development

Environmental protection and sustainable development are interconnected concepts aimed at preserving the planet's natural resources, biodiversity, and ecosystems while promoting social and economic well-being for current and future generations. As human activities impact the environment, it becomes crucial to strike a balance between meeting present needs and ensuring a sustainable future. Let's explore these concepts in more detail:

Environmental Protection:

1. Conservation of Natural Resources: Environmental protection involves conserving natural resources such as air, water, forests, and minerals to ensure their availability for future generations and maintain ecological balance.

2. Biodiversity Preservation: Protecting biodiversity is essential to sustain ecosystems, as diverse species play vital roles in maintaining ecological stability and supporting human life.

3. Pollution Control: Measures to control air, water, and soil pollution are essential to safeguard human health, ecosystems, and biodiversity.

4. Climate Change Mitigation: Environmental protection also includes efforts to address climate change by reducing greenhouse gas emissions and promoting sustainable energy sources.

5. Environmental Laws and Regulations: Governments enact laws and regulations to protect the environment, ensuring responsible use of natural resources and holding polluters accountable.
6. Ecosystem Restoration: Restoration efforts aim to rehabilitate degraded ecosystems, re-establishing their ecological functions and benefits.

Sustainable Development:

1. Long-Term Perspective: Sustainable development involves meeting present needs without compromising the ability of future generations to meet their needs.
2. Social Equity: Sustainable development recognizes the importance of social equity and ensuring that economic growth benefits all members of society.
3. Economic Viability: Sustainable development promotes economic growth that is environmentally responsible and benefits communities and industries alike.
4. Resource Efficiency: Efficient resource use minimizes waste and optimizes resource allocation to reduce environmental impacts.
5. Integration of Goals: Sustainable development seeks to integrate environmental, social, and economic goals in decision-making processes.
6. Global Cooperation: Given the interconnected nature of environmental challenges, sustainable development requires international cooperation and collective action.

Interplay between Environmental Protection and Sustainable Development:

1. Conservation and Sustainable Use: Environmental protection involves conserving natural resources,

while sustainable development focuses on their responsible use to ensure their availability for future generations.

2. Environmental Impact Assessment: Sustainable development practices include conducting environmental impact assessments to understand potential ecological consequences before implementing development projects.

3. Green Technologies: Sustainable development encourages the adoption of green technologies that reduce environmental harm, promoting eco-friendly practices.

4. Circular Economy: A circular economy approach emphasizes reducing, reusing, and recycling resources, minimizing waste, and promoting sustainability.

5. Climate Action: Both environmental protection and sustainable development emphasize climate change mitigation and adaptation to protect ecosystems and communities.

6. Social and Environmental Justice: Combining environmental protection and sustainable development can address social and environmental injustices, ensuring that vulnerable communities are not disproportionately affected by environmental degradation.

Achieving a balance between environmental protection and sustainable development requires collaboration among governments, businesses, communities, and individuals. By working together and implementing responsible practices, societies can foster a harmonious relationship with the environment, promote social well-being, and create a sustainable future for all.

Electoral Systems and Political Representation

Electoral systems play a crucial role in shaping political representation and the functioning of democratic societies. They determine how votes are translated into seats in legislative bodies and, consequently, how diverse interests and perspectives are represented in the government. Different electoral systems can produce distinct outcomes in terms of political representation, party dynamics, and the ability of citizens to influence decision-making. Let's explore how electoral systems influence political representation:

1. Proportional Representation (PR):

In PR systems, political parties are awarded seats in proportion to the percentage of votes they receive in an election. PR systems aim to ensure that parties' seat shares reflect their popular support, allowing for a more accurate representation of diverse political views.

Advantages:

- Diverse Representation: PR often leads to multi-party systems, where a broader range of political ideologies and interests are represented in parliament.
- Minority Representation: PR can enhance the representation of minorities and small parties, ensuring their voices are heard in decision-making.

Disadvantages:

- Less Stable Governments: PR systems may result in coalition governments, which can lead to slower decision-making and compromises among parties.
- Weaker Constituency-Representative Link: In some PR systems, representatives are chosen from party lists rather than specific geographic areas, potentially reducing the direct connection between constituents and their representatives.

2. First-Past-the-Post (FPTP):

FPTP is a single-member district system where candidates with the most votes in individual constituencies win seats. The party or coalition with the most seats typically forms the government.

Advantages:

- Stable Governments: FPTP often produces strong majority governments, allowing for faster decision-making and policy implementation.
- Simple Ballot: FPTP ballots are straightforward, with voters selecting one candidate in their constituency.

Disadvantages:

- Winner-Takes-All: FPTP can result in a winner-takes-all scenario, where the party with the most votes gains a disproportionate number of seats, potentially underrepresenting minority voices.
- Disproportional Outcomes: FPTP may lead to a disconnect between the percentage of votes a party receives and the number of seats it obtains in parliament.

3. Mixed Electoral Systems:

Mixed electoral systems combine elements of PR and FPTP. Voters may have two ballots—one for a candidate in their local district (FPTP component) and one for a political party (PR component). Seats are allocated based on both the individual districts and the overall proportion of votes received by each party.

Advantages:

- Balance between Proportional and Local Representation: Mixed systems attempt to combine the strengths of both PR and FPTP, promoting both local representation and diverse party representation.
- Potential for Diverse Political Landscapes: Mixed systems can lead to varied party dynamics, fostering political competition and representation.

Disadvantages:

- Complexity: Mixed systems can be more complicated for voters to understand, as they involve two different ballots and allocation methods.
- Potential for Electoral Thresholds: Some mixed systems may have electoral thresholds, requiring parties to achieve a minimum percentage of the vote to gain seats, which can impact smaller parties.

It is essential to recognize that each electoral system has its merits and challenges, and the choice of an electoral system can significantly impact political representation and the democratic process. Decisions on electoral systems should consider the unique characteristics and needs of each country or jurisdiction to promote effective and inclusive political representation.

Judicial Review and the Role of the Courts

Judicial review is a fundamental principle of constitutional law that grants courts the authority to review the constitutionality and legality of legislative and executive actions. It allows the judiciary to serve as a check on the other branches of government, ensuring that their actions are consistent with the constitution and the rule of law. The concept of judicial review is closely tied to the idea of constitutional supremacy, where the constitution is the highest law of the land, and all government actions must conform to its provisions. Let's explore the role of the courts in judicial review:

1. Interpreting and Applying the Constitution:

One of the primary roles of the courts in judicial review is to interpret and apply the constitution to specific cases. When a law or government action is challenged as unconstitutional, the court analyzes the relevant constitutional provisions and determines whether the law or action complies with them.

2. Protecting Constitutional Rights:

Judicial review allows the courts to protect and uphold constitutional rights, ensuring that individuals' fundamental liberties are not violated by government actions or laws. Courts act as guardians of these rights, holding the government accountable for any infringement.

3. Ensuring Separation of Powers:

By exercising judicial review, the courts help maintain the separation of powers among the three branches of government (executive, legislative, and judiciary). They ensure that each branch acts within its constitutionally defined authority and that no branch becomes overly dominant or abuses its power.

4. Striking Down Unconstitutional Laws:

If a court finds a law or government action unconstitutional, it has the authority to invalidate or "strike down" the law, rendering it null and void. This power helps prevent laws that infringe on constitutional rights from being enforced.

5. Checking Executive Actions:

Courts can review the actions of the executive branch, including those of government officials and agencies, to ensure that they act within the bounds of the constitution and the law. This helps prevent executive overreach and abuse of power.

6. Assessing Legislative Acts:

Courts can review laws passed by the legislature to determine whether they align with the constitution. This review can be triggered by a legal challenge brought before the court or initiated by the court itself.

7. Preserving the Rule of Law:

Judicial review reinforces the rule of law by holding government actions accountable to constitutional principles. It promotes consistency, predictability, and fairness in the legal system.

8. Safeguarding Democracy:

By serving as a check on government actions, judicial review helps protect the democratic values of a society and ensures that the government operates within constitutional limits.

9. Balancing Rights and Public Interests:

Courts engage in a delicate balance between protecting individual rights and upholding the public interest. They carefully weigh the potential impact of their decisions on society while ensuring that fundamental rights are not unduly restricted.

It is important to note that judicial review is not without its critics. Some argue that it can be undemocratic, as unelected judges can overrule decisions made by elected representatives. However, proponents of judicial review argue that it is a vital safeguard against the tyranny of the majority and a crucial mechanism for upholding the rule of law and protecting individual liberties. Ultimately, the role of the courts in judicial review is a critical aspect of constitutional democracies, ensuring a system of checks and balances and upholding the principles of constitutionalism.

Doctrine of Judicial Review and its Limitations

The doctrine of judicial review is a foundational principle in constitutional law, granting courts the authority to review and invalidate laws, executive actions, or government decisions that are deemed unconstitutional. While this power is essential for upholding the supremacy of the constitution and protecting individual rights, it also has certain limitations and potential drawbacks. Let's explore the doctrine of judicial review and its limitations:

Doctrine of Judicial Review:

1. Basis in Constitutional Supremacy: Judicial review is based on the concept of constitutional supremacy, where the constitution is the highest law of the land, and all government actions must comply with its provisions.

2. Check on Government Actions: The doctrine allows the judiciary to serve as a check on the other branches of government (executive and legislative) by ensuring that their actions conform to the constitution.

3. Protecting Individual Rights: Judicial review helps safeguard fundamental rights by preventing the government from infringing upon them through laws or policies that violate constitutional guarantees.

4. Interpretation of the Constitution: Courts play a crucial role in interpreting and applying the constitution to specific cases, providing clarity on the

meaning and scope of constitutional provisions.

Limitations of Judicial Review:

1. Judicial Activism vs. Restraint: Judicial review can lead to a debate between judicial activism, where courts take an assertive role in shaping public policy, and judicial restraint, where courts are more deferential to the decisions of elected officials. Critics argue that excessive activism can lead to judicial overreach and undermine the democratic process.

2. Counter-Majoritarian Difficulty: Critics also point out the "counter-majoritarian difficulty" in judicial review, as unelected judges may overturn decisions made by elected representatives. Some argue that this undermines the democratic principle of majority rule.

3. Limited Enforcement Power: Courts lack the ability to enforce their decisions independently. They rely on the cooperation of the other branches of government and the public's willingness to comply with their rulings.

4. Lack of Political Accountability: Judges are appointed or elected through a process that aims to maintain their independence and impartiality. However, this lack of direct political accountability can be viewed as a limitation when their decisions have significant policy implications.

5. Subjectivity in Interpretation: Judicial review relies on the interpretation of the constitution by judges, which can be influenced by their personal beliefs and values. This subjectivity can lead to differing interpretations and contentious decisions.

6. Remedies and Delay: Court decisions can take time, and the remedies they offer, such as striking down a law, may not fully address the harm caused by unconstitutional actions.

7. Difficulty in Amending the Constitution: In some cases, judicial review may be seen as an obstacle to constitutional change, as amending the constitution often requires significant political consensus and effort.

Balancing Act:

Balancing the benefits of judicial review with its limitations is a complex task. Courts must exercise restraint and consider the broader implications of their decisions while upholding the rule of law and protecting individual rights. Critics and proponents continue to debate the appropriate role and scope of judicial review in democratic societies, and the conversation remains an essential aspect of constitutional jurisprudence.

The Impact of Judicial Decisions on Public Policy

Judicial decisions can have a profound impact on public policy, influencing the development, interpretation, and implementation of laws and regulations. Courts play a crucial role in shaping public policy through their decisions in various ways:

1. Interpretation of Laws and the Constitution:
   - Courts interpret laws and constitutional provisions to determine their meaning and scope. These interpretations can provide clarity on the intent of legislation and guide policymakers in implementing the law effectively.

2. Setting Legal Precedents:
   - Judicial decisions create legal precedents that serve as guiding principles for future cases with similar issues. These precedents become part of the body of case law, which shapes how laws are interpreted and applied in subsequent cases.

3. Striking Down Unconstitutional Laws:
   - When courts find laws or government actions to be unconstitutional, they may invalidate or "strike down" those provisions, rendering them unenforceable. This can lead to changes in public policy and require lawmakers to revise or replace the unconstitutional provisions.

4. Promoting Individual Rights and Civil Liberties:
   - Judicial decisions can uphold and protect individual

rights and civil liberties, ensuring that public policies respect and preserve fundamental freedoms for all citizens.

5. Influencing Government Action:
- Courts can influence government actions and policies through their decisions on issues such as environmental protection, healthcare access, education equity, and civil rights.

6. Addressing Social and Political Issues:
- Judicial decisions can address pressing social and political issues, such as voting rights, marriage equality, discrimination, and privacy, shaping the trajectory of public policy in these areas.

7. Impact on Public Administration:
- Court decisions can influence how government agencies and departments implement and enforce laws, leading to changes in administrative practices and policies.

8. Encouraging Legislative Action:
- When courts identify gaps or shortcomings in existing laws, their decisions can prompt legislative bodies to enact new laws or amend existing ones to address the issues raised by the court.

9. Balancing the Powers of Government:
- Through judicial review, courts serve as a check on the powers of the legislative and executive branches, ensuring that their actions are consistent with constitutional principles and the rule of law.

10. Public Perception and Advocacy:
- High-profile court decisions can raise public awareness of specific issues, generating public debate and advocacy efforts that may further influence public policy discussions and outcomes.

It is essential to note that the impact of judicial decisions on public policy is not uniform and can vary depending on the political climate, the nature of the issue, the level of public and political support for a particular policy, and the willingness of policymakers to act on court decisions. Moreover, courts' influence on public policy must be balanced with the principle of separation of powers, as the ultimate responsibility for policy decisions rests with the elected branches of government. Nevertheless, the judiciary's role in shaping public policy underscores its significant impact on the development and evolution of the legal and policy landscape in democratic societies.

Court Interpretation of Constitutionally Protected Rights

Court interpretation of constitutionally protected rights is a crucial aspect of judicial review and constitutional law. Courts play a central role in defining the scope and application of rights enshrined in a country's constitution. Their decisions can shape the protection and exercise of these rights, ensuring that they remain relevant and effective in changing societal contexts. Here are key aspects of court interpretation of constitutionally protected rights:

1. Balancing Tests: Courts often employ balancing tests to determine the extent of rights protection in specific cases. These tests weigh the importance of the right against competing societal interests or government objectives. For example, the courts may balance the right to free speech against considerations of public safety or national security.

2. Evolving Standards: Courts' interpretation of rights can evolve over time to reflect changing social norms and values. They consider contemporary understandings of the rights in light of evolving societal perspectives.

3. Scope and Limitations: Courts define the scope of rights and their limitations. They clarify when and under what circumstances certain rights may be restricted or limited, such as in cases of public interest, public order, or national security.

4. Horizontal and Vertical Application: Courts determine

whether constitutional rights apply to actions by private individuals (horizontal application) or only to government actions (vertical application). They may hold private actors accountable if they violate constitutionally protected rights.

5. Overlapping Rights: Constitutional rights can sometimes overlap or come into conflict. Courts resolve such conflicts by carefully balancing the rights at stake and finding solutions that best protect the underlying principles.

6. Consistency with International Law: Courts may draw on international human rights law and treaties to interpret constitutionally protected rights. They often consider relevant international standards and norms to enrich their understanding of these rights.

7. Original Intent vs. Living Constitution: Judges may consider the original intent of the framers when interpreting the constitution, seeking to understand how they intended the rights to be protected. On the other hand, some judges follow the concept of a "living constitution," adapting the interpretation to modern realities and contemporary values.

8. Remedies and Enforcement: When a court finds that a right has been violated, it may order appropriate remedies or relief to protect the affected individual or group. The court's decisions can also influence public policy and government practices related to rights protection.

9. Precedent and Stare Decisis: Courts often rely on past decisions and established legal principles (precedent) to guide their interpretation of constitutionally protected rights. The principle of stare decisis encourages courts to respect previous decisions and maintain consistency in their rulings.

10. Public Discourse and Education: Court decisions on constitutionally protected rights can stimulate public

discourse and raise awareness of these rights. This can lead to greater public understanding and engagement with constitutional issues.

Court interpretation of constitutionally protected rights is an ongoing and dynamic process that continually shapes the meaning and scope of fundamental liberties. Through their decisions, courts act as guardians of these rights, safeguarding them against infringement and ensuring their enduring relevance in a changing society.

Protection of Human Rights and Social Justice

The protection of human rights and the pursuit of social justice are interconnected and essential goals in building fair, inclusive, and compassionate societies. Human rights are inherent to all individuals, regardless of their background, and they encompass fundamental freedoms and dignities. Social justice, on the other hand, seeks to address systemic inequalities and promote equitable access to opportunities and resources. Let's explore how the protection of human rights and the pursuit of social justice are interconnected:

1. Universal Human Rights Framework: Human rights are universal, indivisible, and interdependent. They are enshrined in international human rights instruments such as the Universal Declaration of Human Rights (UDHR) and various human rights treaties. The protection of human rights forms the basis for social justice initiatives, ensuring that all individuals are treated with dignity and respect.

2. Right to Equality and Non-Discrimination: The principle of equality lies at the core of human rights and social justice. Upholding the right to equality ensures that all individuals have equal opportunities to participate in society, regardless of their race, gender, religion, ethnicity, or socio-economic status.

3. Access to Basic Needs and Services: Social justice aims to eliminate disparities in access to basic needs and essential services such as education, healthcare,

housing, and clean water. Ensuring equal access to these resources promotes human dignity and well-being.

4. Empowerment and Inclusion: Human rights and social justice initiatives focus on empowering marginalized and vulnerable populations, providing them with the tools, knowledge, and resources to participate fully in society and decision-making processes.

5. Protecting Civil and Political Rights: Human rights encompass civil and political rights, such as the right to free speech, assembly, and participation in political processes. These rights form the basis for advocating for social justice and holding governments accountable.

6. Economic, Social, and Cultural Rights: Social justice advocates for the protection of economic, social, and cultural rights, such as the right to education, adequate food, and social security. Ensuring these rights are respected promotes equality and reduces poverty and inequality.

7. Combating Discrimination and Prejudice: The protection of human rights involves combating discrimination and prejudice in all its forms. Social justice initiatives work to challenge stereotypes and biases that perpetuate inequalities.

8. Accountability and Rule of Law: Both human rights and social justice rely on accountability mechanisms and the rule of law to ensure that rights are respected, and justice is served.

9. Advocacy and Awareness: Promoting human rights and social justice often involves advocacy, raising awareness, and fostering public support for policies and practices that advance equality and fairness.

10. International Cooperation: Addressing human rights and social justice issues often requires international

cooperation and collaboration among nations and organizations to tackle global challenges collectively.

The protection of human rights and the pursuit of social justice are ongoing processes that require the commitment and engagement of governments, civil society, individuals, and international bodies. By working together to protect and promote human rights and social justice, societies can build a foundation for equality, respect, and dignity for all individuals, creating a more just and inclusive world.

Economic, Social, and Cultural Rights

Economic, social, and cultural rights (ESCR) are an essential category of human rights that focus on securing individuals' well-being and quality of life. Unlike civil and political rights, which emphasize individual liberties and freedoms, ESCR are concerned with ensuring equitable access to basic needs, social services, and opportunities for all individuals, regardless of their socio-economic status. These rights are recognized in international human rights instruments and aim to promote social justice and address systemic inequalities. Let's explore the key aspects of economic, social, and cultural rights:

1. Right to Education: The right to education ensures that everyone has access to quality education at all levels, without discrimination. It encompasses access to primary and secondary education, vocational training, and higher education, promoting opportunities for personal development and advancement.

2. Right to Health: The right to health emphasizes access to healthcare services, including medical treatment, preventive care, and essential medicines. It seeks to achieve the highest attainable standard of physical and mental health for all individuals.

3. Right to Adequate Food and Nutrition: This right entails access to sufficient, safe, and nutritious food that meets individuals' dietary needs and preferences, ensuring freedom from hunger and malnutrition.

4. Right to Housing: The right to housing guarantees access to adequate and safe housing, which includes

secure tenure, habitable conditions, and affordability. This right aims to protect individuals from homelessness and inadequate shelter.

5. Right to Work and Fair Labor Practices: The right to work ensures access to opportunities for decent work, fair wages, safe working conditions, and protection against exploitation. It encompasses the right to form and join trade unions to collectively bargain for workers' rights.

6. Right to Social Security: The right to social security entails access to social protection programs, such as unemployment benefits, pensions, and disability support, to provide a safety net during times of need.

7. Right to Culture and Cultural Participation: This right recognizes the importance of cultural identity and participation in cultural life. It aims to preserve and promote diverse cultural expressions and heritage.

8. Right to Participation in Cultural and Artistic Life: This right emphasizes access to and participation in the arts, culture, and scientific advancement, promoting creativity and intellectual development.

9. Right to Participate in Scientific Progress and Benefit from Scientific Advancements: This right entails access to and participation in scientific endeavors and the benefits of scientific advancements, promoting scientific knowledge and innovation for the benefit of all.

10. Right to Water and Sanitation: The right to water and sanitation ensures access to clean and safe drinking water and adequate sanitation facilities, promoting public health and well-being.

These rights are interrelated and interconnected, and their fulfillment is essential for individuals' dignity and full realization of their potential. Governments have the responsibility to respect, protect, and fulfill economic, social, and cultural rights through policies, programs, and legal measures. International human rights bodies and civil society play a vital role in monitoring and advocating for the realization of these rights on both national and global levels. By safeguarding and advancing economic, social, and cultural rights, societies can work towards a more just, inclusive, and equitable world for all individuals.

Rights of Vulnerable Populations: Women, Children, Minorities, etc.

The rights of vulnerable populations, including women, children, minorities, and other marginalized groups, are an essential focus of human rights advocacy and social justice efforts. These populations often face multiple intersecting forms of discrimination and are more susceptible to human rights violations. Ensuring the protection and promotion of their rights is crucial to building inclusive, equitable, and compassionate societies. Here are some key aspects of the rights of vulnerable populations:

1. Women's Rights:
   - Gender Equality: Promoting gender equality and eliminating discrimination against women in all spheres of life, including education, employment, and political participation.
   - Ending Gender-Based Violence: Protecting women from all forms of violence, including domestic violence, sexual harassment, and human trafficking.
   - Reproductive Rights: Ensuring access to comprehensive reproductive healthcare, family planning, and maternal health services.
2. Children's Rights:
   - Right to Education: Ensuring access to quality education for all children, regardless of their social or economic background.
   - Protection from Exploitation: Protecting children from child labor, child marriage, and other forms of

exploitation.

- Right to Health and Safety: Ensuring access to healthcare, nutrition, and safe living conditions for children.

3. Minority Rights:

- Protection from Discrimination: Guaranteeing the rights of minorities to equal treatment and protection from discrimination based on ethnicity, religion, or language.
- Preservation of Culture: Recognizing and promoting the cultural rights and identities of minority groups.
- Political Participation: Ensuring the participation and representation of minorities in the political process.

4. Indigenous Peoples' Rights:

- Right to Land and Resources: Recognizing and protecting the ancestral lands and resources of indigenous peoples.
- Cultural Rights: Upholding the right of indigenous peoples to maintain and develop their cultural traditions and heritage.
- Free, Prior, and Informed Consent: Ensuring that decisions affecting indigenous communities are made with their full consent and participation.

5. LGBTQ+ Rights:

- Right to Non-Discrimination: Protecting individuals from discrimination based on their sexual orientation, gender identity, or gender expression.
- Right to Safety: Ensuring protection from violence and harassment based on LGBTQ+ status.
- Recognition of Relationships: Advocating for legal recognition and protection of same-sex relationships.

6. Refugees and Migrants' Rights:

- Right to Asylum: Ensuring the protection of refugees fleeing persecution or conflict.
- Right to Dignity: Upholding the rights and dignity of migrants, regardless of their status, and protecting

them from exploitation.
7. Persons with Disabilities' Rights:
- Access to Services and Accommodations: Ensuring access to education, employment, and public services for persons with disabilities.
- Right to Participation: Promoting the active participation and inclusion of persons with disabilities in all aspects of society.

Efforts to protect the rights of vulnerable populations involve legal and policy reforms, advocacy, awareness-raising, and the creation of supportive social and institutional structures. Governments, international organizations, civil society, and individuals all play crucial roles in advancing the rights of vulnerable populations and creating a more just and equitable world for everyone.

Intersectionality of Rights and Multiple Discrimination

The intersectionality of rights and multiple discrimination is a concept that recognizes the overlapping and interconnected nature of various forms of discrimination experienced by individuals who belong to multiple marginalized groups. It acknowledges that individuals may face discrimination based on multiple aspects of their identity, such as race, gender, ethnicity, religion, disability, sexual orientation, socio-economic status, and more. The concept of intersectionality highlights the unique and complex experiences of those at the crossroads of different forms of discrimination, which can amplify the challenges they face and create distinct barriers to the enjoyment of their human rights. Here are key aspects of intersectionality of rights and multiple discrimination:

1. Overlapping Forms of Discrimination: Intersectionality acknowledges that discrimination is not experienced in isolation. Instead, individuals may experience discrimination based on multiple intersecting characteristics, which can magnify the impact of discrimination on their lives.
2. Cumulative Disadvantages: Multiple discrimination can lead to cumulative disadvantages, where individuals face compounded barriers that are greater than the sum of the challenges faced by each marginalized group separately.
3. Unique Experiences: Individuals at the intersection of different marginalized identities may have unique

experiences that are not fully captured by examining each identity in isolation. Their experiences are shaped by the interplay of multiple factors, which can significantly impact their access to opportunities and resources.

4. Invisibility and Marginalization: Intersectionality challenges the tendency to overlook the experiences of individuals with multiple marginalized identities, who may face invisibility and marginalization within society.

5. Complex Identity: The concept of intersectionality recognizes that identity is complex and multifaceted, and individuals' experiences are shaped by the interconnections between various aspects of their identity.

6. Implications for Human Rights: The intersectionality of rights has implications for the protection and promotion of human rights. It emphasizes the need for an inclusive and comprehensive approach to address discrimination and inequality, recognizing the unique experiences of diverse individuals.

7. Policy and Advocacy: Efforts to address intersectionality and multiple discrimination require targeted policies and advocacy that consider the specific needs and challenges faced by individuals with intersecting marginalized identities.

8. Inclusive Data Collection: Collecting disaggregated data based on multiple identity characteristics is essential to better understand the experiences and challenges faced by individuals at the intersection of multiple marginalized groups.

9. Empowerment and Representation: Empowering individuals with intersecting marginalized identities and promoting their representation in decision-making processes are crucial steps in addressing multiple discrimination.

10. Human Rights Approach: Taking an intersectional human rights approach involves recognizing and addressing the ways in which different forms of discrimination intersect and interact, and developing responses that uphold the dignity, equality, and human rights of all individuals, regardless of their identity.

By embracing an intersectional lens, societies can work towards a more inclusive, equitable, and just world that acknowledges and respects the unique experiences and rights of all individuals, regardless of their intersecting identities.

Constitutional Law and Emerging Challenges

Constitutional law faces numerous emerging challenges in the modern world, driven by technological advancements, globalization, shifting social norms, and evolving political landscapes. These challenges test the resilience and adaptability of constitutional frameworks, requiring thoughtful responses to protect fundamental rights, maintain democratic principles, and ensure the rule of law. Some of the key emerging challenges in constitutional law include:

1. Technology and Privacy Rights: Advancements in technology, such as artificial intelligence, biometrics, and data collection, raise concerns about privacy rights. Constitutional law must grapple with how to balance the benefits of technological innovation with protecting individuals' right to privacy.

2. Cybersecurity and National Security: The increasing reliance on digital infrastructure raises challenges related to cybersecurity and national security. Constitutional law must address issues of government surveillance, data breaches, and protecting citizens from cyber threats while upholding civil liberties.

3. Social Media and Freedom of Expression: The rise of social media platforms has revolutionized communication, but it also raises questions about the boundaries of free speech and the responsibilities of tech companies in regulating online content.

4. Disinformation and Fake News: The spread of

disinformation and fake news poses challenges to democratic processes and public discourse. Constitutional law must address how to protect freedom of expression while combating harmful misinformation.

5. Climate Change and Environmental Rights: Climate change presents unprecedented challenges to the environment and public health. Constitutional law must consider the right to a healthy environment and the role of governments in addressing climate-related threats.

6. Migration and Refugee Rights: Global migration patterns and refugee crises challenge constitutional law in addressing issues of borders, asylum, and the rights of migrants and refugees.

7. Economic Inequality and Social Justice: Rising economic inequality and social disparities require constitutional law to consider measures to address these issues, such as progressive taxation and social welfare policies.

8. Globalization and Sovereignty: Globalization blurs traditional notions of sovereignty and raises questions about how constitutional systems can effectively address global challenges while safeguarding national identity and governance.

9. Indigenous Rights and Reconciliation: Constitutional law must grapple with issues related to indigenous rights, land claims, and reconciliation efforts in the aftermath of colonialism and historical injustices.

10. Public Health Crises: The emergence of public health crises, such as pandemics, highlights the need for constitutional frameworks to address emergency powers and the protection of public health while safeguarding civil liberties.

11. Challenges to Democratic Institutions: Constitutional law faces challenges from rising populism, erosion of

democratic norms, and threats to the independence of democratic institutions like the judiciary and media.

Addressing these emerging challenges requires creative legal solutions, public engagement, and a commitment to upholding the principles of constitutionalism and human rights. Courts, legislatures, civil society, and citizens play essential roles in shaping constitutional responses to these complex issues and ensuring that constitutional systems remain robust and adaptive in the face of evolving global realities.

Constitutionalism in the Digital Era

Constitutionalism in the digital era refers to the application and adaptation of constitutional principles and values to the challenges and opportunities presented by the digital age. As advancements in technology continue to transform society, constitutional systems around the world are grappling with how to safeguard fundamental rights, protect democratic principles, and regulate the digital realm. Here are some key aspects of constitutionalism in the digital era:

1. Protection of Privacy Rights: The digital era has brought about new challenges to privacy rights, with increased data collection, surveillance, and cybersecurity risks. Constitutional systems must ensure that privacy rights are protected in the face of technological advancements and government and corporate data practices.

2. Freedom of Expression in Online Spaces: Constitutionalism must address the complexities of freedom of expression in the digital realm. Balancing the need for an open and inclusive internet with the regulation of harmful content and disinformation is a critical challenge.

3. Cybersecurity and National Security: The digital era has seen a rise in cyber threats and attacks, challenging constitutional systems to strike a balance between ensuring national security and protecting civil liberties.

4. Internet Governance and Sovereignty: Globalization and the borderless nature of the internet pose

challenges to traditional notions of national sovereignty. Constitutional systems must navigate the complexities of regulating online activities while respecting international norms and agreements.

5. Digital Rights and Inclusivity: Constitutionalism must ensure that digital rights, such as access to the internet and digital services, are recognized as essential elements of citizenship and that efforts are made to bridge the digital divide.

6. Artificial Intelligence and Algorithmic Accountability: The use of artificial intelligence and algorithms raises questions about accountability and transparency in decision-making. Constitutionalism must address the implications of algorithmic decision-making on individual rights and societal values.

7. Digital Democracy and Civic Engagement: The digital era offers new opportunities for civic engagement and participation in democratic processes. Constitutional systems must embrace digital democracy while safeguarding against disinformation and manipulation.

8. E-Government and Administrative Efficiency: Digital technologies can enhance administrative efficiency and public service delivery. Constitutionalism should ensure that e-government initiatives respect privacy rights and maintain accountability and transparency.

9. Online Dispute Resolution and Access to Justice: The digital era presents opportunities for enhancing access to justice through online dispute resolution mechanisms. Constitutional systems must consider how these mechanisms align with principles of due process and fair representation.

10. Digital Human Rights Education: Constitutionalism should promote digital human rights education to ensure that individuals understand their rights and responsibilities in the digital space.

Constitutional systems face the task of adapting traditional legal principles to the rapidly evolving digital landscape while upholding the rule of law and protecting fundamental rights. Navigating the complexities of the digital era requires an ongoing dialogue among governments, legal experts, technology companies, civil society, and citizens to shape constitutional responses that promote a just, inclusive, and rights-respecting digital society.

National Security and Civil Liberties

The relationship between national security and civil liberties is a complex and delicate balance that constitutional democracies must navigate. National security refers to the protection of a nation's sovereignty, territorial integrity, and citizens from external and internal threats. On the other hand, civil liberties are fundamental rights and freedoms that individuals possess, often enshrined in constitutions, which protect them from government interference and uphold their dignity and autonomy. Balancing these two objectives is critical to maintaining a free and democratic society. Here are some key aspects of the relationship between national security and civil liberties:

1. Surveillance and Privacy: National security measures, such as surveillance programs, are sometimes necessary to prevent and investigate threats. However, such measures can raise concerns about privacy rights, as excessive surveillance may infringe on individuals' right to privacy.

2. Freedom of Expression and Information: In the interest of national security, governments may impose restrictions on freedom of expression and information dissemination to prevent the spread of sensitive or harmful information. This can create tensions with principles of free speech and the public's right to access information.

3. Due Process and Rule of Law: During times of heightened security concerns, there may be pressures to bypass or limit due process protections, such as

habeas corpus or fair trial rights. Upholding the rule of law and ensuring due process is crucial in safeguarding civil liberties even in the face of security challenges.

4. Anti-Terrorism Legislation: National security concerns often lead to the enactment of anti-terrorism legislation. While necessary to combat threats, such laws must be carefully crafted to prevent abuse and protect civil liberties.

5. Access to Information and Government Transparency: National security interests may restrict access to certain government information. Balancing the need for secrecy with transparency is essential to maintain public trust in government institutions.

6. Profiling and Discrimination: Security measures, such as profiling based on race, religion, or ethnicity, can lead to discrimination and the violation of equal protection rights.

7. Freedom of Association and Assembly: Measures taken in the name of national security may impinge on the freedom of association and assembly, inhibiting peaceful protests and public gatherings.

8. Oversight and Accountability: Strong oversight mechanisms, such as independent courts, legislative bodies, and oversight committees, are crucial to ensuring that national security measures do not unduly infringe on civil liberties and are subject to checks and balances.

9. Emergency Powers: During emergencies, governments may invoke emergency powers to deal with security threats. Safeguards must be in place to prevent the abuse of these powers and to ensure their temporary nature.

10. Public Trust and Social Cohesion: The respect for civil liberties while addressing national security concerns is vital to maintaining public trust in government

institutions and fostering social cohesion.

Balancing national security and civil liberties requires ongoing dialogue, transparency, and a commitment to upholding the rule of law. It is essential to recognize that strong protection of civil liberties can strengthen national security by upholding the values and principles that underpin a democratic society. Striking the right balance is an ongoing challenge, and democratic nations must continuously assess and refine their policies and practices to ensure the protection of both national security and civil liberties.

Responses to Global Crises: Pandemics, Climate Change, etc.

Global crises, such as pandemics and climate change, require coordinated and robust responses at the national, regional, and international levels. These crises present complex challenges that transcend borders and demand collective action to safeguard public health, address environmental degradation, and protect the well-being of present and future generations. Here are some key responses to global crises:

1. Pandemics:
   - Preparedness and Early Detection: Building robust public health systems and surveillance capabilities to detect and respond to infectious disease outbreaks promptly.
   - International Cooperation: Collaborating with other nations and international organizations to share information, resources, and best practices in disease prevention and control.
   - Vaccine Development and Distribution: Investing in research and development to create vaccines and ensuring equitable access to vaccines globally.
   - Public Health Messaging: Communicating accurate and timely information to the public to promote preventive measures and reduce the spread of diseases.
2. Climate Change:
   - Mitigation Strategies: Implementing policies to reduce greenhouse gas emissions, transition to renewable energy sources, and promote sustainable practices in

various sectors.

- Adaptation Measures: Developing and implementing adaptation strategies to cope with the impacts of climate change, such as extreme weather events and rising sea levels.
- International Agreements: Participating in global agreements, like the Paris Agreement, to collaborate on climate action and emission reduction targets.
- Public Awareness and Education: Raising awareness about climate change and engaging the public in sustainable practices and conservation efforts.

3. Global Health and Environmental Governance:

- Strengthening International Institutions: Supporting and strengthening global health and environmental institutions to coordinate responses to crises effectively.
- Resource Mobilization: Ensuring adequate funding and resources to address global health and environmental challenges.
- Equity and Inclusivity: Prioritizing the needs and voices of vulnerable populations and developing countries in crisis responses.

4. Disaster Management:

- Preparedness and Risk Reduction: Investing in disaster preparedness and risk reduction measures to minimize the impact of crises like natural disasters and extreme weather events.
- Emergency Response and Relief: Coordinating rapid responses to provide aid, relief, and support to affected communities during and after crises.

5. Technological Innovation:

- Harnessing Technology: Leveraging technological advancements, data analytics, and artificial intelligence to enhance crisis management and response efforts.
- Research and Development: Encouraging research and

innovation to develop new solutions and technologies to address global challenges.

6. Cross-Sector Collaboration:
- Public-Private Partnerships: Promoting partnerships between governments, private sectors, non-governmental organizations, and academic institutions to pool resources and expertise.
- Interdisciplinary Approaches: Encouraging collaboration between diverse disciplines, such as science, medicine, engineering, and social sciences, to address the multifaceted nature of global crises.

7. Long-Term Planning:
- Sustainable Development Goals: Aligning responses to global crises with the United Nations' Sustainable Development Goals (SDGs) to address interconnected challenges and foster long-term sustainability.

Responding to global crises requires a coordinated and multifaceted approach that transcends borders and ideologies. It demands international solidarity, adaptive governance, and the commitment of governments, businesses, communities, and individuals worldwide. By working together and investing in preventive measures and sustainable solutions, societies can build resilience and effectively address the pressing challenges of our time.

Comparative Constitutional Law

Comparative Constitutional Law is a branch of constitutional law that focuses on studying and analyzing the similarities and differences between different constitutional systems and legal frameworks across countries. It involves examining various aspects of constitutions, including their structure, content, interpretation, and implementation, to gain insights into how different nations address similar legal and governance issues. Comparative Constitutional Law aims to understand the strengths and weaknesses of constitutional arrangements and to identify best practices that can inform constitutional reforms and enhance democratic governance worldwide. Here are key aspects of Comparative Constitutional Law:

1. Study of Different Constitutional Systems: Comparative Constitutional Law involves a systematic study of the constitutions of different countries, including written, unwritten, federal, unitary, and hybrid systems, to understand the principles and practices that govern them.

2. Examination of Constitutional Provisions: Legal scholars and experts analyze specific provisions within constitutions, such as separation of powers, fundamental rights, executive authority, and judicial review, to understand how these provisions function and interact in different constitutional contexts.

3. Role of Courts and Judicial Review: Comparative Constitutional Law delves into the role of courts, particularly constitutional courts, in interpreting and safeguarding the constitution. It explores how courts

exercise judicial review and protect fundamental rights.

4. Comparative Methodology: Comparative Constitutional Law uses a rigorous comparative methodology to identify patterns, trends, and variations across constitutional systems. It involves case studies, statistical analysis, and in-depth research to draw meaningful conclusions.

5. Constitutional Change and Reform: By studying different constitutional systems and their historical evolution, scholars can analyze processes of constitutional change, amendments, and reforms, identifying factors that lead to successful or unsuccessful constitutional revisions.

6. Protection of Human Rights: Comparative Constitutional Law examines how various constitutions protect and guarantee human rights, including the influence of international human rights standards on national constitutions.

7. Federalism and Decentralization: The study of Comparative Constitutional Law also delves into federal and decentralized systems, analyzing how power is distributed between central and regional authorities in different countries.

8. Diversity and Pluralism: Comparative Constitutional Law explores how different countries handle issues related to cultural, religious, and ethnic diversity, and how constitutions safeguard the rights of minority groups.

9. Constitutionalism and Rule of Law: This branch of constitutional law also focuses on the principles of constitutionalism and the rule of law, examining how they are upheld or challenged in various constitutional systems.

10. Lessons and Best Practices: Comparative Constitutional Law aims to draw lessons and identify

best practices from successful constitutional models that can be applied to enhance democratic governance and protect fundamental rights in different contexts.

Through Comparative Constitutional Law, scholars, policymakers, and legal practitioners gain a deeper understanding of constitutional systems and the ways in which constitutional frameworks impact governance, human rights, and the rule of law across different countries. This comparative approach fosters an appreciation for the diversity of constitutional experiences and helps in crafting informed and context-specific constitutional reforms and policies.

Analysis of Different Constitutional Systems

Analyzing different constitutional systems involves a comprehensive examination of various aspects of constitutions and governance structures in different countries. By comparing and contrasting different constitutional models, legal scholars, policymakers, and researchers gain valuable insights into the strengths and weaknesses of different systems and identify patterns and trends that can inform constitutional reforms and improve democratic governance. Here are key areas of analysis in comparing constitutional systems:

1. Constitutional Structure: Analyzing the structure of constitutions involves studying the form and organization of constitutional documents, such as written or unwritten constitutions, and identifying the main components, such as the preamble, articles, and amendments procedures.

2. Form of Government: Comparing different constitutional systems helps in understanding the form of government, such as parliamentary, presidential, or hybrid systems, and the distribution of powers between different branches of government.

3. Separation of Powers: Analyzing the separation of powers in different constitutional systems involves studying the checks and balances between the executive, legislative, and judicial branches, and how they interact to prevent abuse of power.

4. Head of State and Head of Government: Comparing

the roles and powers of the head of state and head of government in different systems sheds light on their respective functions and responsibilities.

5. Bill of Rights and Fundamental Rights: Studying the inclusion and protection of fundamental rights in different constitutions helps in understanding the level of protection afforded to citizens and the scope of civil liberties and human rights.

6. Judicial Review: Analyzing the role of courts, particularly constitutional courts, in exercising judicial review and interpreting the constitution helps in understanding the strength of the judiciary as a guardian of the constitution.

7. Federalism and Unitarism: Comparative analysis of federal and unitary systems reveals the distribution of powers between central and regional governments and the degree of autonomy granted to subnational entities.

8. Amendment Procedures: Studying amendment procedures in different constitutions provides insights into the flexibility or rigidity of constitutional arrangements and the processes required for constitutional change.

9. Political Party Systems: Analyzing the political party systems in different countries helps in understanding the dynamics of multi-party systems, two-party systems, and the influence of political parties on governance.

10. Protection of Minority Rights: Comparing the protection of minority rights in different constitutional systems highlights the approaches taken to ensure the inclusion and participation of diverse communities in governance.

11. Constitutional Stability and Flexibility: Analyzing the historical stability and adaptability of different constitutions reveals how well they withstand the test

of time and respond to changing societal needs.

12. Role of Citizens and Civic Participation: Comparative analysis of constitutional systems also examines the role of citizens in the democratic process, including the mechanisms for civic participation and engagement in governance.

By analyzing different constitutional systems across countries, scholars gain valuable insights into the diversity of constitutional experiences and the impact of different governance structures on democracy, human rights, and the rule of law. This comparative approach helps in identifying best practices and lessons from successful constitutional models, as well as areas for improvement, guiding efforts to enhance constitutionalism and democratic governance worldwide.

Lessons from International and Regional Human Rights Courts

International and regional human rights courts play a crucial role in interpreting and protecting human rights under international and regional human rights treaties and conventions. These courts issue judgments and rulings on cases brought before them, setting legal precedents and providing guidance to member states on the implementation and enforcement of human rights standards. The lessons learned from these courts can be valuable for advancing human rights protection and promoting the rule of law globally. Here are some key lessons from international and regional human rights courts:

1. Strengthening Human Rights Norms: Human rights courts contribute to the development and strengthening of international and regional human rights norms by interpreting treaty provisions and clarifying the scope and application of human rights.

2. Enhancing Accountability: The courts' rulings hold states accountable for human rights violations, promoting transparency and reinforcing the importance of adherence to international and regional human rights obligations.

3. Fostering Dialogue and Cooperation: The decisions of human rights courts foster dialogue and cooperation between states, human rights institutions, and civil society, creating opportunities for addressing systemic human rights issues.

4. Protecting Vulnerable Groups: Human rights courts often prioritize the protection of vulnerable groups, such as minorities, women, children, refugees, and indigenous peoples, ensuring that their rights are safeguarded against discrimination and marginalization.

5. Addressing Impunity: The courts' rulings play a vital role in addressing impunity for human rights violations, as they require states to investigate and prosecute perpetrators and provide remedies to victims.

6. Balancing National and International Jurisdiction: Human rights courts help strike a balance between national and international jurisdiction, allowing states to address human rights issues domestically while upholding international human rights standards.

7. Strengthening Access to Justice: The courts' decisions contribute to enhancing access to justice for individuals and communities, providing a venue for victims to seek redress for human rights violations.

8. Promoting Rule of Law: By upholding human rights principles, the courts promote the rule of law, ensuring that states comply with their legal obligations and respect human rights as an essential part of good governance.

9. Supporting Institutional Development: Human rights courts support the development of national human rights institutions, providing guidance on the establishment and functioning of effective and independent bodies responsible for human rights protection.

10. Addressing Emerging Human Rights Challenges: The courts' jurisprudence evolves to address emerging human rights challenges, such as new forms of discrimination, technology-related rights issues, and

environmental concerns.

11. Inspiring Advocacy and Awareness: The courts' decisions inspire human rights advocacy and awareness-raising efforts, empowering civil society organizations and individuals to promote and protect human rights.

12. Contributing to Regional and Global Human Rights Dialogue: Human rights courts contribute to regional and global human rights dialogues, fostering cooperation and mutual learning between different human rights systems.

Overall, the lessons from international and regional human rights courts underscore the significance of these judicial bodies in advancing human rights protection, promoting accountability, and upholding the rule of law. By leveraging the insights gained from these courts, governments, civil society, and international actors can work collaboratively to address human rights challenges and foster a more just and rights-respecting world.

The Role of Civil Society and Public Engagement

Civil society and public engagement play a crucial role in shaping democratic governance, promoting human rights, and advancing social progress. Civil society encompasses a wide range of non-governmental organizations, community groups, advocacy networks, and individuals who work collectively to advocate for the public good and hold governments and institutions accountable. Here are key aspects of the role of civil society and public engagement:

1. Advocacy and Awareness: Civil society organizations engage in advocacy to raise awareness about critical social, political, and human rights issues. Through public campaigns, social media, and grassroots activities, they mobilize public support for causes that promote social justice and human rights.

2. Monitoring and Accountability: Civil society acts as a watchdog, monitoring government actions and policies to ensure they align with human rights standards and democratic principles. They provide independent assessments of government performance and advocate for accountability when rights are violated.

3. Participation and Representation: Civil society provides a platform for marginalized communities and underrepresented groups to have a voice in decision-making processes. They promote inclusivity and diversity in public discourse and governance.

4. Service Delivery and Social Welfare: Many civil society organizations deliver essential services and support to vulnerable populations, addressing gaps in government provision and promoting social welfare.

5. Research and Policy Analysis: Civil society organizations conduct research and policy analysis, providing evidence-based recommendations to policymakers and influencing the formulation of laws and policies.

6. Bridge between Citizens and Government: Civil society acts as a bridge between citizens and government, facilitating dialogue and fostering partnerships to address societal challenges collaboratively.

7. Human Rights Advocacy: Civil society plays a vital role in promoting and protecting human rights, advocating for the ratification and implementation of international human rights treaties and conventions.

8. Public Participation in Decision-Making: Public engagement initiatives, such as town hall meetings, public consultations, and participatory budgeting, allow citizens to influence policymaking and contribute to democratic governance.

9. Social and Political Mobilization: Civil society organizations mobilize citizens for collective action, empowering them to participate in social movements and advocate for change.

10. Conflict Resolution and Peacebuilding: Civil society often plays a significant role in conflict resolution and peacebuilding efforts, promoting dialogue, reconciliation, and understanding among diverse communities.

11. Innovation and Grassroots Initiatives: Civil society fosters innovation and grassroots initiatives, empowering communities to find localized solutions to their unique challenges.

12. Capacity Building and Empowerment: Through

training and capacity-building programs, civil society empowers individuals and communities to actively engage in civic life and decision-making processes.

In many democratic societies, civil society and public engagement serve as essential complements to government institutions, contributing to the health and vibrancy of democracy. They enrich public debate, promote transparency, and ensure that governments are responsive to the needs and aspirations of their citizens. A strong and vibrant civil society is a hallmark of inclusive and participatory governance, fostering a sense of ownership and responsibility among citizens for the well-being of their societies.

Importance of Civic Education on Constitutional Rights and Duties

Civic education on constitutional rights and duties is of paramount importance in fostering informed and engaged citizens who actively participate in democratic governance. It plays a crucial role in strengthening the rule of law, protecting fundamental rights, and promoting responsible citizenship. Here are some key reasons why civic education on constitutional rights and duties is vital:

1. Empowering Citizens: Civic education empowers citizens by equipping them with knowledge about their constitutional rights and duties. Informed citizens are more likely to engage in the democratic process, exercise their rights responsibly, and hold government officials accountable.

2. Protecting Democracy: A well-informed citizenry is essential for the functioning of a healthy democracy. Understanding constitutional principles and values helps citizens appreciate the importance of democratic institutions and the rule of law, safeguarding democracy from potential threats.

3. Upholding Rule of Law: Civic education instills respect for the rule of law by educating citizens about the importance of adhering to constitutional principles and abiding by the law. This fosters a culture of legality and reduces the likelihood of constitutional violations.

4. Promoting Active Citizenship: When citizens understand their constitutional rights and duties,

they are more likely to engage in civic activities, such as voting, participating in public debates, and volunteering for community causes.

5. Advancing Social Justice: Civic education helps citizens recognize social injustices and disparities, motivating them to advocate for positive change and uphold the principles of equality and human rights.

6. Encouraging Civil Discourse: Informed citizens are better equipped to engage in civil discourse and respectful debates about societal issues. This promotes an inclusive and pluralistic society where diverse viewpoints are heard and respected.

7. Strengthening Civic Participation: Civic education encourages citizens to participate in civic affairs, including community service, advocacy, and involvement in non-governmental organizations, thereby strengthening civil society.

8. Mitigating Disinformation: An informed citizenry is less susceptible to manipulation and disinformation, reducing the risk of polarization and promoting fact-based decision-making.

9. Preventing Constitutional Ignorance: Ignorance of constitutional rights and duties can lead to abuses of power and violations of human rights. Civic education serves as a bulwark against such violations by increasing awareness of constitutional safeguards.

10. Building Social Cohesion: Understanding constitutional rights and duties fosters a sense of shared values and common purpose, promoting social cohesion and a sense of national identity.

11. Long-term Governance and Stability: Citizens well-versed in their constitutional rights and duties contribute to more stable and sustainable governance, as they are better equipped to participate in electoral processes and advocate for reforms through peaceful means.

12. Future-Proofing Democracy: Civic education ensures that future generations are prepared to uphold democratic principles, protecting democracy for years to come.

Civic education on constitutional rights and duties is not only beneficial to individuals but also to society as a whole. By cultivating an informed and engaged citizenry, it reinforces democratic governance, strengthens human rights protection, and fosters a sense of collective responsibility for the welfare and progress of the nation. As a cornerstone of democracy, civic education empowers citizens to actively participate in shaping their future and the future of their society.

Citizen Participation in Constitutional Reforms

Citizen participation in constitutional reforms is a vital component of inclusive and democratic governance. Involving citizens in the process of amending or drafting constitutions ensures that the resulting document reflects the aspirations and needs of the people it governs. Here are some key reasons why citizen participation is crucial in constitutional reforms:

1. Legitimacy and Public Trust: Citizen participation enhances the legitimacy of the constitutional reform process. When citizens are involved in shaping their constitution, they are more likely to trust and respect the final outcome.

2. Representation and Inclusivity: Constitutional reforms should represent the diverse interests and perspectives of the population. Citizen participation ensures that voices from all segments of society are heard, including marginalized and underrepresented groups.

3. Informed Decision-Making: Engaging citizens in the reform process allows them to be informed about constitutional issues and debates, leading to better decision-making and thoughtful deliberation.

4. Ownership and Commitment: When citizens actively participate in shaping the constitution, they develop a sense of ownership and commitment to the final document, increasing its chances of successful implementation.

5. Checks and Balances: Citizen participation serves as a check on the power of government and constitutional authorities during the reform process, preventing undue concentration of power.
6. Social Cohesion: Involving citizens in constitutional reforms can promote social cohesion by providing a forum for dialogue and mutual understanding among diverse groups.
7. Transparency and Accountability: An inclusive reform process fosters transparency and accountability, as citizens can monitor the decision-making and implementation stages.
8. Conflict Resolution: In countries emerging from conflicts or transitioning from authoritarian regimes, citizen participation in constitutional reforms can promote reconciliation and peacebuilding.
9. Capacity Building: The process of citizen engagement in constitutional reforms can also build civic capacity and awareness of constitutional rights and duties.
10. Long-Term Stability: A constitution crafted through citizen participation is more likely to endure and provide a stable foundation for governance, as it reflects the broad consensus of the population.

Methods of Citizen Participation in Constitutional Reforms:

1. Public Consultations: Holding public consultations, town hall meetings, and forums where citizens can express their views and provide feedback on proposed constitutional changes.
2. Surveys and Feedback Mechanisms: Conducting surveys and using feedback mechanisms to collect public opinions on specific constitutional issues.
3. Citizen Assemblies and Deliberative Forums: Establishing citizen assemblies or deliberative forums composed of randomly selected citizens to discuss and

propose constitutional reforms.

4. Civic Education and Public Awareness: Conducting civic education campaigns to inform citizens about the content and implications of proposed constitutional changes.

5. Online Platforms: Utilizing online platforms and social media to engage citizens in the reform process and collect input.

6. Civil Society Engagement: Working with civil society organizations to facilitate citizen participation and amplify citizen voices.

7. Public Hearings and Submissions: Organizing public hearings and accepting written submissions from citizens and stakeholders.

8. Referendums: In some countries, constitutional reforms are subject to public referendums, giving citizens a direct vote on proposed changes.

Citizen participation in constitutional reforms is a reflection of democratic values and the commitment to inclusive governance. It is a powerful tool to build consensus, ensure accountability, and strengthen the foundations of constitutional democracy. By involving citizens in the reform process, nations can create constitutions that better serve the needs and aspirations of their people and promote a more just and equitable society.

Future Directions of Constitutional Law

The future directions of constitutional law are shaped by ongoing societal, technological, and global developments that continue to impact governance and human rights. As constitutional law adapts to these changes, it will play a crucial role in addressing emerging challenges and shaping the legal landscape. Here are some key future directions of constitutional law:

1. Technological Advancements: Constitutional law will grapple with issues related to digital rights, data privacy, surveillance, and artificial intelligence. The protection of individuals' rights in the digital era and striking a balance between security and privacy will be critical concerns.

2. Environmental Protection: Constitutional law will increasingly address environmental challenges, such as climate change, resource depletion, and ecological degradation. Constitutions may incorporate provisions to safeguard the environment and future generations' rights to a healthy planet.

3. Protection of Vulnerable Groups: Constitutional law will continue to focus on the protection of vulnerable populations, including women, children, minorities, LGBTQ+ communities, and refugees. Ensuring equal rights and combating discrimination will remain crucial issues.

4. Globalization and Supranational Law: As globalization advances, constitutional law will navigate the tensions between national sovereignty and the

influence of supranational institutions and treaties, such as the European Union and international human rights conventions.

5. Strengthening Democracy: Constitutional law will seek to enhance democratic institutions, promote electoral integrity, and address challenges posed by misinformation and disinformation in the digital age.

6. Economic and Social Rights: The future of constitutional law will involve a continued focus on economic and social rights, such as access to education, healthcare, and housing, to ensure that constitutional protections extend to all aspects of human well-being.

7. Emergence of New Rights: Advancements in technology, social progress, and scientific developments may give rise to new rights and challenges that constitutional law must grapple with, such as the right to digital access or environmental rights.

8. Gender and Diversity: Constitutional law will increasingly incorporate gender and diversity perspectives, addressing issues of gender equality, gender identity, and the inclusion of diverse voices in governance.

9. Public Health and Bioethics: In light of global health crises, constitutional law may evolve to include provisions on public health emergencies, bioethics, and medical ethics.

10. Access to Justice and Legal Empowerment: Constitutional law may explore ways to enhance access to justice for all citizens, including legal empowerment initiatives and innovative dispute resolution mechanisms.

11. Climate Migration and Human Rights: Constitutional law will grapple with the challenges of climate-induced migration and the protection of human rights

for climate refugees.

12. Artificial Intelligence and Constitutional Governance: As AI becomes more prevalent, constitutional law may address the implications of AI on governance, rights, and decision-making processes.

Adapting constitutional law to these future directions will require robust legal analysis, judicial creativity, and public engagement. Constitutional scholars, policymakers, and legal practitioners will need to work together to ensure that constitutions remain relevant and effective in safeguarding human rights, promoting democracy, and addressing the evolving needs of society. Embracing these challenges will be essential in shaping constitutional law's future and its capacity to foster just and inclusive societies.

Adapting Constitutional Law to Technological Advancements

Adapting constitutional law to technological advancements is a critical task in the modern era. Rapid technological developments present both opportunities and challenges for constitutional governance, human rights, and the rule of law. To ensure that constitutional frameworks remain relevant and effective, several key considerations and approaches can be taken:

1. Protection of Digital Rights: Constitutional law should explicitly recognize and protect digital rights, such as the right to privacy, data protection, freedom of expression online, and access to information in the digital realm.

2. Balancing Security and Privacy: Constitutions should strike a balance between national security interests and the protection of individual privacy, particularly in the context of surveillance and data collection by the state.

3. Regulation of Emerging Technologies: Constitutional law can empower lawmakers to regulate emerging technologies, such as artificial intelligence, blockchain, and biometrics, to ensure that they are developed and used ethically and responsibly.

4. Internet Governance: Constitutional provisions may address internet governance and the protection of internet freedom, ensuring that governments do not unduly restrict access to information and online

communication.

5. Right to Digital Access: As access to the internet becomes essential for participation in modern society, constitutional law can recognize the right to digital access as a fundamental right.

6. E-Government and E-Democracy: Constitutional law can support the adoption of e-government and e-democracy measures to enhance citizen engagement, transparency, and accountability in governance.

7. Cybersecurity and Cybercrime: Constitutional provisions can establish frameworks for cybersecurity and addressing cybercrime, enabling states to protect critical infrastructure and citizens from digital threats.

8. Technology and Due Process: Constitutional law should ensure that technological advancements do not undermine due process in legal proceedings, such as the use of algorithms in decision-making or automated law enforcement.

9. Digital Inclusivity: Constitutional provisions can promote digital inclusivity, ensuring that technological advancements do not exacerbate existing social and economic disparities.

10. Education and Digital Literacy: Constitutional law can encourage the promotion of digital literacy and education to empower citizens to navigate the digital world effectively and responsibly.

11. Protection Against Online Disinformation: Constitutions may address the issue of online disinformation and establish mechanisms to combat its spread without compromising freedom of expression.

12. Technological Neutrality: Constitutional law can adopt principles of technological neutrality to ensure that legal protections are adaptable to evolving technologies without requiring frequent

constitutional amendments.

13. International and Regional Cooperation: Given the global nature of technology, constitutional law may address international and regional cooperation on digital issues, including data sharing and cybersecurity.

Adapting constitutional law to technological advancements requires a forward-thinking and flexible approach that upholds human rights and democratic principles while embracing the potential of technology to improve governance and society. This process should involve multi-stakeholder consultations, including civil society, experts, and technology innovators, to ensure that constitutional frameworks keep pace with the rapid evolution of the digital age.

Ensuring Constitutional Resilience and Flexibility

Ensuring constitutional resilience and flexibility is essential to enable constitutions to withstand challenges, adapt to changing circumstances, and remain effective over time. Constitutional frameworks should be designed with built-in mechanisms that allow for both stability and adaptability. Here are some key strategies to ensure constitutional resilience and flexibility:

1. Clear and Precise Language: Constitutions should use clear and precise language to articulate foundational principles and rights while allowing for interpretation and evolution over time. Vague or overly rigid language can hinder flexibility.

2. Amendment Procedures: Constitutions should include clear and accessible procedures for amendments, allowing for necessary updates to address societal changes and emerging challenges. However, these procedures should strike a balance to prevent frequent and frivolous changes.

3. Sunset Clauses: Incorporating sunset clauses in certain constitutional provisions can provide a time-bound duration for specific measures or provisions, ensuring periodic review and adaptability.

4. Preambles and Guiding Principles: Preambles and guiding principles in the constitution can set the tone for interpretation and implementation, providing flexibility to address unforeseen circumstances while maintaining the constitution's core values.

5. Interpretation by Courts: The judiciary plays a crucial role in interpreting the constitution. Courts' ability to interpret constitutional provisions in light of contemporary circumstances enhances the constitution's adaptability.

6. Review Commissions: Establishing review commissions or expert bodies to periodically assess the constitution's relevance and effectiveness can identify areas that require updates or reform.

7. Evolving Jurisprudence: Constitutional courts can develop a living jurisprudence that adapts to changing societal norms and values, ensuring the constitution remains relevant to the times.

8. Independent Constitutional Councils: Independent bodies tasked with constitutional review can ensure the constitution's integrity and provide guidance on its interpretation and adaptation.

9. Dialogues and Deliberation: Engaging in national dialogues and deliberation on constitutional issues can involve citizens in the process of identifying necessary reforms and building consensus.

10. Public Participation: Involving the public in the constitutional amendment process fosters ownership and legitimacy, making reforms more resilient to political changes.

11. International and Comparative Law: Taking into account international human rights norms and best practices in constitutional design can enhance a constitution's resilience and adaptability.

12. Gradual Reforms: Incremental reforms can help manage societal changes while preserving the constitution's foundational principles and avoiding abrupt and destabilizing changes.

13. Constitutional Courts' Authority: Strengthening the authority and independence of constitutional courts allows them to serve as guardians of the constitution

and ensure its resilience.

14. Mechanisms for Conflict Resolution: Establishing mechanisms for peaceful conflict resolution within the constitutional framework can prevent crises that may threaten the constitution's stability.

By incorporating these strategies, constitutional framers can strike a balance between resilience and flexibility, ensuring that the constitution remains a living document capable of addressing contemporary challenges while upholding its enduring values and principles. A constitution that is both resilient and flexible is better equipped to protect individual rights, promote democratic governance, and serve as a foundation for a just and inclusive society.

Addressing Challenges in a Globalized World

Addressing challenges in a globalized world requires coordinated efforts at the international, regional, and national levels. As globalization continues to shape the global landscape, nations face a range of complex issues that transcend borders and require collective action. Here are some key approaches to address challenges in a globalized world:

1. Multilateral Cooperation: International collaboration among nations, through organizations such as the United Nations, World Trade Organization, and regional bodies, is crucial to tackle global challenges like climate change, pandemics, terrorism, and migration.

2. Strengthening International Law: Strengthening and upholding international law is essential to provide a framework for addressing transnational issues and promoting peace, security, and human rights.

3. Sustainable Development Goals (SDGs): Nations should work towards achieving the United Nations' Sustainable Development Goals, which address poverty, inequality, environmental protection, and other global challenges.

4. Global Health Initiatives: Collaborative efforts are required to address global health challenges, enhance healthcare systems, and improve access to vaccines and essential medicines.

5. Climate Action: Nations need to cooperate in

combating climate change, reducing greenhouse gas emissions, and protecting biodiversity through initiatives like the Paris Agreement.

6. Addressing Inequality: Globalization has exacerbated income inequality. International efforts to promote inclusive economic growth and address wealth disparities are essential.

7. Trade and Investment Agreements: Responsible and balanced trade and investment agreements can foster economic growth and social development while safeguarding environmental and labor standards.

8. Cybersecurity and Data Protection: Collaborative efforts are needed to address cybersecurity threats, protect data privacy, and establish norms for responsible behavior in cyberspace.

9. Education and Awareness: Global challenges often require informed and educated citizens. Promoting education and awareness about global issues is crucial for building a more engaged and responsible global community.

10. Humanitarian Assistance and Refugee Protection: International cooperation is essential in providing humanitarian aid and protecting the rights of refugees and displaced persons.

11. Promoting Dialogue and Diplomacy: Engaging in dialogue and diplomatic efforts can help resolve conflicts and prevent tensions that may arise in a globalized world.

12. Cultural Exchange and Understanding: Fostering cultural exchange and mutual understanding can build bridges between nations and promote peace and tolerance.

13. Technology Transfer and Capacity Building: Assisting developing nations in technology transfer and capacity building can bridge the digital divide and promote sustainable development.

14. Corporate Social Responsibility: Encouraging businesses to practice social and environmental responsibility can contribute to addressing global challenges.
15. Promoting Rule of Law and Good Governance: Upholding the rule of law and promoting good governance at the national and international levels are fundamental to addressing global challenges effectively.

Addressing challenges in a globalized world requires a shared commitment to cooperation, mutual respect, and finding common ground. Nations must recognize that their fates are intertwined and that collective action is essential for a prosperous and sustainable future for all. Embracing these approaches can pave the way for a more inclusive, resilient, and interconnected global community.

Empowering Democratic Societies through Constitutional Law

Empowering democratic societies through constitutional law is essential to ensure the protection of fundamental rights, promote accountable governance, and foster inclusive participation in decision-making processes. Constitutional law serves as the foundation of democratic systems, defining the rules, institutions, and principles that govern a nation. Here are key ways in which constitutional law empowers democratic societies:

1. Safeguarding Fundamental Rights: Constitutional law enshrines fundamental rights and liberties, such as freedom of expression, assembly, and equality before the law. These rights provide citizens with the tools to express themselves, advocate for their interests, and challenge government actions that infringe upon their liberties.

2. Checks and Balances: Constitutional law establishes a system of checks and balances among different branches of government (executive, legislative, and judiciary). This system ensures that no single branch becomes too powerful and that government actions are subject to scrutiny and accountability.

3. Rule of Law: Constitutional law upholds the rule of law, ensuring that laws and government actions are consistent with the constitution and applicable laws. This principle guarantees that no one is above the law, including government officials, and that legal

processes are fair and transparent.

4. Separation of Powers: Constitutional law divides government powers between different branches, preventing the concentration of authority in one entity. This separation helps prevent abuses of power and fosters a system of checks and balances.

5. Electoral Processes: Constitutional law establishes the framework for electoral processes, ensuring free and fair elections. Regular elections allow citizens to participate in choosing their representatives and holding leaders accountable.

6. Public Participation: Constitutional law can provide mechanisms for public participation in decision-making processes, such as referendums, public consultations, and participatory budgeting. These avenues empower citizens to influence policies and governance.

7. Local Governance: Constitutional law can provide for decentralized and local governance, empowering communities to address their unique needs and participate in local decision-making.

8. Judicial Review: Constitutional courts play a vital role in upholding the constitution's supremacy and protecting citizens' rights. Judicial review allows courts to assess the constitutionality of laws and government actions, ensuring compliance with constitutional principles.

9. Protection of Minorities: Constitutional law can protect the rights of minorities and marginalized groups, ensuring that they have equal opportunities and are not discriminated against.

10. Democratic Culture: Constitutional law fosters a democratic culture by setting the standards for ethical conduct, transparency, and accountability in public service.

11. Access to Justice: Constitutional law guarantees access

to justice for all citizens, enabling them to seek legal redress when their rights are violated.

12. Civil Society Participation: Constitutional law can support civil society organizations' role in advocating for citizens' rights and promoting public accountability.

13. Social Justice: Constitutional law can advance social justice by addressing inequality, poverty, and promoting policies that benefit the entire society.

14. Human Rights Protection: Constitutional law provides a framework for the protection of human rights, including economic, social, and cultural rights, and ensures that governments actively work to fulfill these rights.

Empowering democratic societies through constitutional law requires a commitment to upholding democratic values, respecting human rights, and promoting inclusivity. It is a collective effort involving lawmakers, policymakers, civil society, and citizens working together to build and sustain vibrant, participatory, and accountable democracies.

www.ingramcontent.com/pod-product-compliance
Lightning Source LLC
Chambersburg PA
CBHW072209290526
45794CB00004B/1700